Journalism and Social Media

Diana Bossio

Journalism and Social Media

Practitioners, Organisations and Institutions

palgrave
macmillan

Diana Bossio
Swinburne University
Hawthorn, VIC, Australia

ISBN 978-3-319-65471-3 ISBN 978-3-319-65472-0 (eBook)
DOI 10.1007/978-3-319-65472-0

Library of Congress Control Number: 2017949199

Cover credit: Jetta Productions

Printed on acid-free paper

This Palgrave Macmillan imprint is published by Springer Nature
The registered company is Springer International Publishing AG
The registered company address is: Gewerbestrasse 11, 6330 Cham, Switzerland

Preface

Some concepts used in this book have come from research that I have previously published. None of these publications has been reproduced in part or in total in this book. Discussion of the Arab Spring in Chap. 3 draws upon concepts from the book chapters 'Journalism during the Arab Spring: Interactions and Challenges' and 'War of Worlds? Alternative and Mainstream Journalistic Practices in Coverage of the "Arab Spring" Protests'.

Discussion of the relations between social media managers and journalists in Chaps. 4 and 5 draw upon concepts from the journal article 'Don't Tweet This! How Journalists and Media Organisations Negotiate Tensions Emerging from the Implementation of Social Media Policy in Newsrooms'.

Discussion of journalists' representations of personal and professional identity on social media in Chap. 6 draws upon concepts from the journal article 'From "Selfies" to Breaking Tweets: How Journalists Negotiate Personal and Professional Identity on Social Media'.

These inclusions are referenced in the text of the chapters.

Hawthorn, Australia Diana Bossio

Acknowledgements

I am indebted to a number of people for their support during the research and writing of this book. Firstly, I owe a debt of gratitude to the incredible scholars who took the time to critique drafts of this manuscript. In particular, I must thank Associate Professor Alfred Hermida for reviewing my proposal, as well as Dr. Anthony McCosker, Dr. Renee Barnes, Professor Folker Hanusch, Professor David Domingo and Dr. Avery Holton for providing feedback on drafts of these chapters. Your feedback was invaluable: thank you.

I probably owe my sanity to the staff in the Department of Media and Communication at Swinburne University. Thank you for your support and good grace when I was either especially busy, absent or forgetful during writing and editing. Thanks especially to Peter Marcato and Julian Novitz for picking up some of the administrative slack, and Esther Milne, Lisa Gye, Steven Conway, Cèsar Albarran-Torres, Dan Golding, Rowan Wilken and Anthony McCosker (again!) for their patience and friendship.

The Faculty of Health, Arts and Design at Swinburne University has supported parts of the research in this book, as well as providing time away from my desk, which allowed me to finish writing. My thanks to Dr. Carolyn Beasley for facilitating this support.

Thank you to the editorial and production staff at *Palgrave*, especially Felicity Plester, Heloise Harding and Martina O'Sullivan, for their enthusiasm and professionalism.

To my students for putting up with my 'book brain': I thank you, I am sorry and I will reply to your emails.

My eternal gratitude to my mum and dad, for everything really, but especially for their encouragement, advice and food delivery service this year. Thanks also to my brothers and their partners for their support and *Instagram* likes.

To my best friends, Anna, Melissa, Penny and Natasha, whom I have missed terribly while living in the 'book cave' for the past year. Thank you for cheering me on and putting up with my absences.

Thank you to the people who have had to live with me while I wrote this book, especially to Alyssia and Angelina, who have made me laugh and kept me up to date with the best baby animal memes.

It would be remiss of me not to thank my cat, Evie, the worst writing partner ever and co-creator of my *Facebook* series, 'Reasons I Can't Work at Home'. Please get off my laptop.

Finally, to Troy, for three very important contributions to this book. Firstly, thank you for gifting me your art. Secondly, thank you for your contribution to the book's conceptual framing, though I will probably never know if journalism 'is' or 'ism'. Lastly, thank you for your love and support. It means everything.

Contents

CHAPTER 1

Journalism and Social Media: An Introduction

It's 1997 and you are starting a typical workday as a print journalist. You arrive at the newsroom and grab the day's newspapers to check the headlines. You greet colleagues from the separate online and newspaper teams and then check your landline for messages. You talk to the chief of staff about the day's events, and after the morning's editorial meeting, your day is organised around getting to media events, talking to sources on the phone and following up potential leads. You will submit up to ten stories for publication in the newspaper by the late afternoon, which might later be 'shovelled' onto the news website. You love your job, but you've heard a lot of worrying things about the future of newspapers. Cadetship entry to the newspaper has been slashed this year, new jobs are scarce and the future of classified and commercial advertising revenue looks uncertain. A lot of journalists are talking about re-skilling or moving on to professional communication roles, and overall the industry is feeling the tension of an uncertain future.

Now fast-forward 20 years to 2017.

Your typical workday as a journalist starts the moment you wake up. You check your smartphone, clicking immediately on *Facebook*, *Twitter*, *Instagram* and *Snapchat* to look at a mix of personal and media-related profiles. Over breakfast, you check content that has already been posted by your news organisation and compare it with what is trending. You post a few comments on your personal *Twitter* profile, which has 1000 followers. Then you switch to your separate professional *Twitter* profile, which has 8000 followers, and share a few links to your media

D. Bossio, *Journalism and Social Media*,
DOI 10.1007/978-3-319-65472-0_1

organisation and post a quick snap of your breakfast. Once you get to work, you greet the small team—mass redundancies in the mid-2000s have resulted in a lean organisation, and your colleagues now work across print, online and social media. Newspaper operations have been largely scaled back, with fewer pages, more lifestyle content picked up from freelance labour and the publication of more syndicated news. Low cadet numbers are now funnelled into video and mobile content roles, where numbers have doubled. A major media event means you will take responsibility for live updates on both the organisation's *Twitter* account, as well as 'express news' on the website. You might only work on two or three stories, but you will be responsible for updating them constantly, optimising both for lunch and commute-time reading on mobile devices. You love your job, but you're concerned that your attention is increasingly divided, and that your professional labour extends into your personal time. Overall, the industry is feeling the tension of being in transition—the opportunities for online and social media reportage seem exciting, but no one knows how these opportunities will translate into 'professional journalism'.

There are only two things that have not changed since journalism entered into social media environments—the durability of journalism as a profession and the uncertainty of its future. When the possibilities for online journalism were beginning to be realised more than 20 years ago, traditional journalism was seen to be under threat. Online news creation and distribution shifted journalists and their audiences away from the traditional 'one-way' communication model typified by newspaper and broadcast journalism. Citizen and other 'non-professional' news content creation, information abundance and new online-enabled technologies increasingly characterised news reportage (Livingstone and Asmolov 2010), leading to pressure on journalists to be multiskilled and engaged across platforms (Cremedas and Lysak 2011; Saltzis and Dickinson 2008). Classified and commercial advertising revenue suffered a sharp downturn and job cuts meant increased productivity pressures on journalists, who were asked to publish news and opinion in more formats and more quickly than ever before. This industrial tumult led some to predict the 'death' of journalism (Altheide 1994) and the dominance of amateur, opinion and tabloid journalism.

While the doomsday predictions have faded, there remains much uncertainty about journalism: what it should look like, who should do it, and what its norms of practice should be. The introduction of social media to journalistic work came at a time when journalism was already in a state of transition. In the 'Web 1.0' phase, journalists and news organisations adjusted to the demands of the 24-hour newsroom, and re-skilled to create multiplatform content and streamlined newsrooms. But then social media's popularity exploded. Coupled with the technological advances in smartphones and tablets, social media is now where audiences are predominantly posting, finding and sharing news and information. 'Web 2.0' has meant sociality; websites and blogs gave way to micropublishing, short messages, geolocational sharing, image dominance and a focus on individual engagement. Stories became 'viral' through individual 'likes' or the popularity of an issue, trend or hashtag. Just when journalists thought they understood online news reportage, social media changed the rules.

Social media platforms and their associated characteristics, politics and cultures are becoming increasingly influential in the production and distribution of news. This book explores some of the changes that the use of social media has brought to journalism, focussing on its impacts on individual professional practice, organisational processes and roles, and the larger institutional understanding of journalism as a profession. I argue that the impact of social media on journalism can be seen through the complex and interconnected relations, practices and professional boundaries that seek both to innovate and delimit the ways in which social media can be used in a news context. Thus, the role of social media platforms in the changing professional landscape of journalism is discussed both in terms of the changes brought to journalistic practice, and the way in which journalistic use of social media has impacted on particular uses of these platforms.

The aims of this book are to:

- Critically analyse the new challenges and opportunities that have emerged for practitioners, organisations and the profession overall as a result of the increasing use of social media in journalism;
- Understand how these changes influence, and are influenced by, the interconnections between individual practitioners, audiences, organisations and larger institutional norms; and finally,
- Use these understandings to provide a conceptual framework with which to understand the ways in which the constitution of journalism itself is changing in social media environments.

The conceptual approach of the book is not simply to describe changed journalistic practices, but also to encapsulate a complex relationship of technical, organisational and institutional influences that have occurred due to the increasing use of social media to investigate, produce and distribute news. This approach foregrounds journalistic use of social media as part of dynamic processes based on relationships in particular social, professional and organisational contexts, rather than solely the consequences of corporate or technological changes and trends (García et al. 2009). Thus, the larger institutional understanding of journalism and how it is constituted can be analysed as a result of the many different individual and organisational influences on its institutional boundaries as a profession.

Much of the research conducted about social media use by journalists or news organisations has focussed on the new practices used to find, research and present the news (Sacco and Bossio 2017; Domingo et al. 2008). Researchers have analysed social media use in journalism primarily as a way to increase audience participation and dialogue (Hermida and Thurman 2008; Sheffer and Schultz 2009) or to distribute content instantaneously (Messner et al. 2012). Other studies have investigated the potential of social media as a new form of journalism (Heinrich 2011; Hirst and Treadwell 2011; Hjort et al. 2011). Some research has also centred on journalists' professional identities and associated values and norms in relation to social media (Lewis and Westlund 2015; Lasorsa et al. 2012). While this research has already shown the positive and negative impacts of social media on 'doing' journalism (Diakopoulos et al. 2012), less attention has been given to the wider transitions occurring across the journalism as an institution—the ways journalists, their organisations and institutions have been impacted by and, conversely, impact the use of social media platforms. Less attention has been paid to the relations between various journalistic 'stakeholders', whether they are managerial, editorial, or the global audiences with an interest in journalistic use of social media. Similarly, the myriad institutional changes occurring as journalists' professional mission, routines, and relationships with audiences go through significant and dynamic transformation have rarely been discussed in detail. Thus, journalism scholars and students will benefit from an exploration of the interrelations between the individual practitioners, the organisational structures and policies, as well as the larger institutional norms and ideologies that frame journalism. *Journalism and Social Media* reflects on the specific contexts in which these three areas of journalism both intersect and interact.

This approach is admittedly ambitious in its scope and, of course, cannot analyse every interconnected influence on contemporary mainstream journalism practice. There are many topics that are important to the study of journalism that cannot be covered in this book, not least the issue of how and whether professional journalism will exist in the future. This book does not have the scope to make predictions about the future of journalism, such as theories for improved business models, or social media practices that might support professional journalism in future. Instead, the book aims to forward a kind of 'history of the present', illustrating some aspects of individual practice, organisational frameworks and institutional ideologies that indicate how journalists and journalism are transitioning into social media environments. Furthermore, the use of case studies and examples in this book is meant to be illustrative of arguments made in individual chapters, but cannot be generalised to journalism practice overall. At the very least, resistance and innovation in changing media environments should illustrate the complexity of individual professional, organisational and cultural changes in journalism. Indeed, focussing on the complexity of these interconnections means this book is neither celebratory nor pessimistic about the changes that social media has brought to professional journalism, nor deterministic about the influences and uses of social media affordances overall.

Defining the Everyday Norms of Journalism

This book focusses on the everyday practices of professional journalism in the western, liberal tradition: the decisions, relationships and practices that connect to produce daily news content. Much of the research about journalism and social media does not focus on the everyday, ordinary practices of news work; instead, extraordinary media events or highly innovative journalistic practices are foregrounded as an illustration of the transformative potential of social media. While this is of course, important, this book suggests that the transformation of journalism can be seen in the daily use of social media that either extend or limit various organisational and institutional structures, policies and professional boundaries. Extraordinary events such as the Arab Spring or the #Blacklivesmatter movement bring innovative examples of the importance of social media to the larger aspirations for news is production and distribution. However, the approach of this book concerns itself with everyday uses of social media to achieve a more nuanced understanding of journalism in transition—that is, the ways social media affordances and cultures have been influenced and negotiated at the everyday level of news production.

This book focusses on journalism practised by 'professional journalists': those whose professional practice is based on paid news work—finding, researching, reporting and disseminating news on various platforms for a news or media content-focussed organisation. Much debate exists about the defining characteristics of journalism; it has been variously called a craft, a profession and an ideology. Indeed, the boundaries between what constitutes 'true' journalism have always been, and will continue to be, blurred (Carlson and Lewis 2015). Following Deuze (2005, p. 446), I define professional journalism as an occupational ideology, which typifies norms of practice and behaviours that structure professional work and validate a particular social status. This ideology provides the framework for journalism as a social institution and the privileged social status journalists claim to represent news to audiences. In this book, the distinction of professional journalism is not intended to create a hierarchical division from some of the excellent amateur, citizen, activist and unpaid journalism that is occurring online and on social media (see Bebawi and Bossio 2014, for further discussion of these types of journalism). Rather, the focus on professional, paid journalism allows further investigation of the everyday organisational, professional and institutional structures that regulate and delimit the use of social media. At times, this book will also refer to 'legacy' or 'mainstream' media or journalism, mostly to create an opposition between workers and organisations that are historically and contextually framed by a one-way broadcast model of news production, and the newer digital, online and social media-focussed organisations and practices. While this book focusses on the transition of professional, paid and mostly traditional legacy journalism practices and organisations, empirical evidence within the chapters is sourced from a number of different news contexts; examples of professional journalism can be found within legacy news organisations, like the *BBC*, as well as smaller disruptors, like *Vice*.

In the context of journalistic practice, 'everyday' refers to the mostly short-form, non-specialised, daily reportage conducted by journalists in local, regional, metropolitan and, in some cases, international contexts. This might also mean everyday reportage on an issue that has some global currency, such as climate change or a political scandal. It is the kind of reportage that journalists might consider the regular part of their practice or 'news round'. This definition is framed by Raymond Williams' theorisation of culture as 'ordinary'; the creative practices of journalism and use of tools such as social media are part of the daily, communal, ritualised labour of making sense of everyday life (Williams 1958, p. 6). According to Williams (1958, p. 8), the daily practices of culture are 'active'—that is, practices like journalism are part of a process of learning and then reflecting on what constitutes the community, and are thus open to negotiation and change. Similarly, Highmore (2011, p. 6) positions the everyday as an active process where social and cultural practices go from 'unusual' to 'regular' (and sometimes back again). In the context of journalism, this book investigates the processes, relationships and practices that are impacted by the transition of social media into a state of 'becoming ordinary' within journalistic practice (Bossio and Bebawi 2016).

Defining Social Media

Social media can be defined as web-based applications or services that exist to allow a series of connections to be made online through a profile or media content. Social media thus allows individuals or groups of users to: (1) construct and share a particular representation of identity or events online through a public or semi-private social networking profile and content creation; (2) view, share or discuss particular content or social connections with other users; and (3) view the content and connections of others with online profiles (boyd and Ellison 2007). The popularity of social media platforms began to emerge in the late 1990s with platforms like *Friendster*, but did not gain mainstream, popular usage until the early 2000s, with the large-scale adoption of *MySpace* (and later, *Facebook*) by a mostly youth-based audience (boyd and Ellison 2007; van Dijk 2013). The creation of a wide array of platforms and services has ensued, offering web tools that have created or augmented communication abilities. A range of brands and organisations—such as *Facebook*, *Twitter*, *YouTube* and *Instagram*—has become synonymous with activities such as microblogging, chatting, or video and image sharing (van Dijk 2013, p. 7).

Journalistic use of social media through news sharing sites or 'social news' was initially popularised by platforms such as *Digg* and *Newsvine*, types of social bookmarking sites dedicated to sharing news and information. By the early 2000s, most news organisations had established websites and audience sharing of news content appeared to be a 'natural' extension of news distribution practices. This is not to suggest that the advent of social media has been trouble-free. *MySpace* never recovered its initial popularity after a $580 million acquisition by *News Corporation* in 2005 (Lynley 2011), *Facebook* and *Instagram* have faced difficulty changing any of the characteristics of their platforms without vehement user dissent, and *Twitter* has been consistently plagued by rumours of 'imminent death' through loss of active users (Tsukayama 2016). Like many social media companies, *LinkedIn*'s stock fortunes have also risen and waned exponentially, indicating that while many social media tools are innovative, their business practices may not be (Gara 2016).

The increasing influence of social media on journalism is understood in this book through both its technical and social affordances. Understanding affordances represents a relational approach to understanding how people interact with social media technologies (Leonardi 2013). Following Evans et al. (2017), this book posits affordances as 'possibilities for action…between a technology and the user that enables or constrains potential behavioural outcomes in a particular context'. Importantly, these affordances are not deterministic; instead, changing abilities and contexts impact on outcomes for use of technologies. There is not a single method of understanding social media affordances—the social use of each platform has encouraged a particular culture, politics and etiquette that has resulted in ever-evolving communication styles. As more platforms have emerged, other differences have appeared within modes of publishing, distribution and audience response. As boyd and Ellison suggest (2007, p. 210), many social media platforms maintain pre-existing social networks, while others help to connect strangers through various communication tools. Social media connections can be made through shared interests, links, commercial activity, political or social groupings or coordinated activities. Social media platforms also provide opportunities for broader commentary on current events, through the processes of linking, as well as possibilities for users to add their own perspective as informal and even humorous contributions to discussion of news events. This might occur in the form of links to other voices and reportage, or the creation of memes and humorous hashtags. While early iterations of social media platforms were focussed on individual expression and creating networks, newer formats have seen increased opportunities to create and share original content. Many of these and other characteristics of social media have had impacts on social and professional relationships amongst other spheres of social life.

The presentation and distribution models of particular social media platforms have had an enormous impact on news and information and, by extension, the constitution of journalism. In the context of journalism, social media's technical affordances have influenced a number of collaborative, participatory and networked behaviours and practices within the research, production and distribution of news. The increasing importance of social media to news consumers has influenced news production values, including: increasing prioritisation of the interactivity of news content, participation of audiences in news, transparency in news production processes, and immediate, 24-hour dissemination of news on social media (Usher 2014). In this book, I conceptualise the unique impact of social media on journalism through understanding of its specific technologies, relations, politics, languages and etiquettes. This creates both a unique 'culture of communication', and a unique environment in which to produce and distribute news. This can be seen in increased sharing and collaborative activities, as well as broader negotiation of journalistic authority in the public sphere. I focus on the impact of three related aspects of social media's communication culture on journalism: the empowerment of audiences, cultures of collaboration and sharing and, finally, the prioritisation of authenticity in communication.

The empowerment of audiences is central to understanding social media communication cultures. Allen (2005, p. 18) suggests that the South Asian tsunami in 2004 was one of the decisive 'moments' in 'social' journalism, where hundreds of images, videos and other media created by people living through the crisis were the most prominent aspect of the news coverage, shared both with news organisations and through social media platforms. Similarly, the *BBC* reported that in the wake of terrorist bomb attacks on the underground train system in 2005, the organisation received 22,000 emails and text messages with information about the bombings. In the first hour alone, they received 50 of the 3000 images they would then go on to use in reportage (Douglas 2006). Most global news organisations like *CNN*, *BBC* and *Al Jazeera* now have dedicated teams to manage the huge volume of user-generated content they receive each day during news events. Journalists and their news organisations have also extended this use of 'citizen journalism' by trying to focus on engagement with individual users or 'followers' about particular issues and events through use of social media. While the public has always actively engaged with media (Ang 2006; Fiske 1987), social media changes the nature of public participation in the news process. Contemporary mainstream journalism now 'competes' with alternative provision of news facilitated by the low cost and availability of digital media and social media platforms, which empower citizens to participate actively in the making of news by creating, shaping and sharing information about news.

Using social media enables and empowers audiences to be more involved in the process of creating and shaping news; they can choose to become users and co-producers in collaborative or participatory processes of creating news (Harrison and Brea 2009; Heinonen 2011; Hermida 2010). Relations based on sharing allow production and distribution of news and information that prioritises the iterative, dialogic and diverse nature of social media communication. Thus, an important part of this sharing and collaboration is individual expression. The use of affect, opinion and emotion, rather than objectivity or neutrality, is seen as a way to ensure a more authentic engagement with social media audiences. Providing an authentic representation of identity is a way of eschewing the supposedly 'elitist' broadcast model of objective distance from the audience. Cultures of audience dominance, sharing and authenticity have developed as unique characteristics of social media communication, and will continue to develop as new roles, relations and rules of engagement are negotiated between different social media users. Thus, as the importance of social media for news and information production and dissemination increases, so too does the need to conceptualise the opportunities and limits of social media affordances for professional journalism and its stakeholders.

Understanding Social Media and Journalistic Practice

Much has already been written in academia and in the media about the changes that have occurred to journalistic production, consumption and reception in digital, online and, now, social media-enabled communication environments. Many scholars have described both the challenges and opportunities that social media bring to journalistic practice (Deuze 2003; Hermida 2010). For example, O'Sullivan and Heinonen (2008, p.

357) have shown that social media bring additional tools to journalism that increase opportunities for interactivity and audience engagement. Others (Hermida 2010; Bebawi and Bossio 2014) have described examples where media-savvy journalists have utilised social media to report news stories during war or crisis and to engage with witnesses when governmental or official accounts are not reliable representations of the day's events. Conversely, other research has problematised journalistic use of social media by showing that many journalists still tend to conform to traditional norms of practice even when using new media platforms (Hermida 2012). Much of this reluctance stems from issues of privacy and verification, which have also been shown to undermine journalists' willingness to participate on social media (Cision 2009). Similarly, some journalists have sometimes been reluctant to use social media in crisis situations, as the lack of source anonymity has provided identification data to governmental forces aiming to neutralise online dissenters (Fuchs et al. 2012).

Descriptions of the positive and negative implications of social media use by journalists are productive in understanding the ways in which it has been implemented in everyday practice. However, these opportunities and challenges occur within a framework of complex influences that journalists are attempting to balance in this time of transition in their professional practice. On the one hand, some journalists do seek to 'normalise' traditional modes of journalistic professional identity, such as objectivity and neutrality, in an online space. On the other hand, many journalists are also seeking ways to utilise a more personal or 'authentic' tone and expanded potential for participation engendered by communication cultures on social media. Between these needs, journalists also negotiate editorial, organisational and institutional influences to have an 'authentic' presence online (Bossio and Sacco 2016). This book seeks to understand these influences as the basis for analysing the ways in which social media has affected—and been effected by—journalistic practice.

Perhaps the most obvious change that social media has brought to journalistic production and practice is to the relationship between the audience and the individual journalism practitioner. A journalists' role in the public sphere has been traditionally represented as a one-way broadcast of news and information to a largely passive audience, a privileged role in which an individual journalist sourced and selected the evidence they deemed to be meaningful to the news agenda. By the late 1950s, journalists were represented as 'gatekeepers' for the public, 'the ones who decide what the public needs to know, as well as when and how such information should be provided'. (Domingo et al. 2008, p. 326). News outlets justified journalists' privileged role by pointing to their responsibility to provide objective, verifiable and high-quality information (Domingo et al. 2008).

The positive implications of this audience engagement on social media are the apparent democratisation and pluralisation of the institution of journalism—the more people involved in the investigation, production and dissemination of news, the better opportunities for information to be disseminated to global audiences. This collaborative turn in the journalistic process has been articulated as 'participatory' journalism, describing the phenomenon of participation in and contribution to the gathering, selection, publication, dissemination and interpretation of news (Deuze et al. 2007; Domingo et al. 2008). Bruns (2006) calls the paradigm shift from industrial to participatory media production 'produsage', where 'the production of ideas takes place in a collaborative, participatory environment which breaks down the boundaries between producers and consumers and instead enables all participants to be users as well as producers of information and knowledge' (Bruns 2006, p. 2). This type of journalism combines organisational production and communal 'produsage' (Bruns 2010) in that both the public and journalists participate in the production as well as the consumption of information. Indeed, much contemporary academic research has been focussed on the innovative uses of social, digital and online media in journalistic practice to formulate new ways of interacting and presenting news to audiences, who are now also seen as collaborators and 'credible sources' (Bowman and Willis 2003).

While these examples illustrate how social media might assist global audiences or witnesses in gaining access to journalists, the incorporation of social media into the everyday reporting practices of mainstream journalists has been a much more recent—and complex—phenomenon. Much of the research described assumes a social media-savvy journalist and newsroom; however, previous research has certainly shown that neither journalists, nor their media organisations, appear to fully understand and utilise social media as an innovative way of presenting content, nor as a way to engage more fully with audiences. For example, Standley (2013, pp. 143–144) found that many traditional news organisations were only using the delivery function of social media—the 'social', or audience engagement, component was almost absent from reportage. Some contemporary studies have shown that some news organisations have invested resources and hired experts to optimise their social media presence (Parr 2009), but others have shown that use of social media and online innovation more broadly has been constrained by problems of poor editorial integration, legal issues and organisational constraints (Newman 2009). Journalists do not appear to be 'early adopters' of social media. However, there are a number of factors that may be impacting on their use of social media. To understand these influences and limitations, the conceptual lens must be widened to include the organisational, editorial and managerial impacts of the newsroom and its stakeholders on individual journalistic use of social media.

Understanding Social Media and the News Organisation

While many theoretical models describe changes to individual journalistic practices, these changes also need to be analysed as part of the larger organisational effects on journalism and its products. Much academic research illustrates that journalistic outlets worldwide have now integrated social media into news reporting (Posetti 2009), though there are variations in the strategies that organisations have used. Some use social media as a supplementary communication channel enabling journalists to cover a distant event in real time, and others to find 'exemplars or eyewitnesses' (Heinonen 2011, pp. 38–39). The *ABC* news network in Australia, for example, utilises social media for emergency and disaster communication, 'gathering and disseminating emergency information quickly and to a vast potential "audience"' (Posetti and Lo 2012, p. 38). Similarly, *Al Jazeera* has used social media to invite users to submit content that is then published on its citizen journalism platform, *Sharek* (Lavrusik 2011). In these collaborative initiatives, journalists take on a 'dialogical' (Heinonen 2011) and 'curatorial' approach (Hermida 2012), encouraging citizens to contribute to the storytelling process as well as navigating, examining, selecting and contextualising user-generated text, photos and videos (Bell 2011; Katz 2011). Other media organisations are much more promotional in their use of social media, encouraging journalists to foster links with audiences through personal or professional social media engagement that links back to the organisations' web presence. Many organisations also manage journalists' use of social media through training and policies, as well as promotional use of individual profiles. By participating on social network platforms as an individual, rather than simply posting content through a media organisation, a journalist is portraying a 'personal brand'. Most news organisations encourage branded use of social media by individual journalists because they are more prominent in online discussions than the news organisation itself (Bruns 2012, p. 105). Audiences are also said to prefer to follow individual rather than institutional social media accounts (Hermida 2013). Media organisations are therefore keen to 'piggyback' on the profiles of individual journalists and do so by linking specific organisational strategies to individual journalistic practice.

While organisational factors do influence individual practice through the individual's adherence to organisational strategies for news dissemination and production, as well as through compliance with social media policies, journalists' professional use of social media is more often influenced by institutional norms of practice. Journalists engage in promotion of their own 'personal brand' as a way to develop professional credibility (Holton and Molyneux 2015). Some journalists have embraced the opportunity to present something of their personal and social selves to reflect the authenticity that characterises social media communication (Lasorsa et al. 2012). However, balancing institutional ideologies, organisational pressures, and maintaining a sense of online authenticity creates what Marwick and boyd (2011, p. 126) describe as 'context collapse'—the sheer diversity of the audience complicates how a public persona or identity can be managed. If being 'personal' is crucial in building a 'brand', yet authenticity is key to the believability of this brand (Marwick and boyd 2011), journalists must negotiate multiple audiences by strategically creating posts that portray an authentic, yet broadly engaging, personality (Marwick and boyd 2011, p. 122). In this context, the institutional influence on the norms and boundaries governing how a journalist can represent themselves on social media is especially important.

Understanding Social Media and Journalism as an Institution

The norms and values that indicate journalistic professional practice are discursively constructed and 'performed' to maintain a particular character that only a professional journalist can be seen to possess; for example, the content of higher education journalism degrees suggests personal characteristics such as independence, detachment and desire to uncover truth as important to the professional work of journalists (De Burgh 2003, p. 109). Professional journalism is thus articulated through a particular mode of behaviour and values through which the journalist can represent themselves and their work (Johnstone et al. 1976). For example, behaviours such as objectivity, verification and individual autonomy are seen as integral to journalism's social authority and often frame organisational codes of conduct. These behaviours have also been institutionalised as the core of journalism and reified as central to the gatekeeping and agenda-setting role of journalism. For a journalist, this also means balancing editorial, organisational and institutional demands on how and what a professional journalist should present online. In this way, journalists understand the institution of journalism as deriving meaning and significance from ideological representation of their work. As Revers (2014, p. 49) suggests, journalists participate in the narratives ingrained in their occupational tradition. They also rely on these collective representations when they define normative principles and perform the behavioural boundaries of their work (Revers 2014, p. 50).

At times, the industry and academic discussion of journalism in a social media-enabled age can often be seen to take on a binary approach—the ideal of a collaborative, transparent process of audience engagement versus a normative, journalist-centred process of production (Bossio and Sacco 2016). But the use—ideal or otherwise—of social media by journalists is much more complex than this binary suggests. Indeed, a sole conceptual focus on journalistic practice, instead of the complex interaction between individual, organisational and institutional perspectives, can often exacerbate the reliance on a 'traditional conceptual lens' (Mitchelstein and Boczkowski 2009, p. 563). Instead this book seeks to illustrate a much more complex state of transition in contemporary journalism, where journalists are attempting to balance the institutional and organisational pressures of 'being online' with their own professional norms and expectations.

Chapter Summary

This book comprises eight chapters, with each focussing on either the individual practitioner, the contemporary journalism organisation or the institutional ideologies and norms framing the journalistic profession. The case studies in this book illustrate the material consequences of balancing these tensions while attempting to transition their professional activity into social media environments. The divisions between the journalism practitioner, organisation and institution are, of course, constructed for purposes of clarity; indeed, the central premise of this book is to illustrate the interconnections between practitioners, organisations and the institution of journalism. The book begins by focussing on individual practitioners and their professional experiences in social media environments. Chapter 2, 'Social Media and Journalism Practice', explores how journalism practices are influenced by the use of social media in reportage. Focussing on three traditional norms of journalistic practice—objectivity, verification, and professional autonomy—this chapter describes how these important professional traits have been continually challenged by social media cultures of communication that prioritise representation of authenticity, transparency and collaborative production. Some of these characteristics have contributed to increasing innovation in the way journalists have both researched and presented the news online; however, this chapter also shows that the transition of journalistic practice to social media environments also comes with organisational and institutional challenges. Chapter 3, 'Journalism and Social Media Audiences', explores the relationship between journalists and news audiences through interactions in social media environments. While much academic research has focussed on how online audiences have impacted the production and distribution of news, this chapter focusses more broadly on the ways that public dialogue between journalists and audiences has incorporated more iterative, collaborative and distributed forms of social media communication. This illustrates that it is not only journalistic practice that is changing, but also the culture of communication between journalists and audiences, which affects the framework for professional journalism's importance in social life.

The next part of the book moves from an individual practitioner's perspective to an organisational perspective on journalistic use of social media. The chapters focus on exploring the new social media-focussed relationships, policies and processes in the newsroom that impact overall production and distribution of news. Chapter 4, 'Social Media and the Newsroom: New Relationships, New Policies, New Practices', explores the transition of journalistic production and distribution of news from an organisational perspective, in particular the new professional relationships, policies and procedures that have been introduced to govern both the individual and organisational use of social media in the newsroom. This chapter illustrates that although there is much variation in the ways that newsrooms have attempted to integrate social media use into the newsroom, the important relationships between journalistic, editorial and management staff determine whether integration of social media in the newsroom is successful. Chapter 5, 'Big Data, Algorithms and the Metrics of Social Media News', focusses on the increasing organisational use of social media analysis and algorithmic manipulation in the production and distribution of news. This chapter illustrates that news organisations are increasingly using social media platforms and analytics to improve the distribution of news content, but they are also increasingly competing with other stakeholders hoping to influence the way news discourses are represented.

The final part of the book takes a broader view of journalism as a professional institution—the norms, practices and boundaries that make up a contemporary understanding of journalism and how these are shifting in a social media age. Chapter 6, 'Shifting Values, New Norms: Social Media and the Changing Profession of Journalism', illustrates some of the material consequences of balancing individual, organisational and professional norms while attempting to transition journalistic professional activity onto social media. In particular, this chapter focusses on the ramifications of these changes on the way journalists see themselves—their professional identity and the institution through which they conduct professional work. Finally, Chap. 7, 'News in Social Media Environments: Journalism in a "Post-Truth" World', considers the changes brought by social media to understanding of journalism as a mode of distributing news and information. This chapter illustrates that the use of social media has influenced new modes of producing and distributing news, which has resulted in the decentralisation of the journalist and news organisation from the communication of news.

References

Allen, S. (2005). *Citizen journalism: Global perspectives.* New York: Peter Lang Publishing.

Altheide, D. L. (1994). Postjournalism: Journalism is dead, long live journalism! The Gulf War in perspective. *Fulbright Papers, 13,* 134.

Ang, I. (2006). *Living room wars: Rethinking media audience for a postmodern world.* London: Routledge.

Bebawi, S., & Bossio, D. (2014). *Social media and the politics of reportage: The Arab spring.* London: Palgrave.

Bell, M. (2011, July 3). Andy Carvin: The Middle East revolutions one tweet at a time. *The Washington Post*. Retrieved from http://voices.washingtonpost.com/blog-post/2011/03/andy_carvin_the_middle_east_re.html.

Bossio, D., & Bebawi, S. (2016). Mapping the emergence of social media in everyday journalistic practices. *Media International Australia, 161*(1), 147–158.

Bowman, S., & Willis, C. (2003). We media: How audiences are shaping the future of news and information. *The Media Center at the American Press Institute*. Retrieved from http://www.hypergene.net/wemedia/.

boyd, d., & Ellison, N. (2007). Social network sites: Definition, history and scholarship. *Journal of Computer-Mediated Communication, 13*(1), 210–230.

Bruns, A. (2006). Towards produsage: Futures for user-led content production. In F. Sudweeks, H. Hrachovec, & C. Ess. (Eds.), *Proceedings of cultural attitudes towards communication and technology* (pp. 275–284). Tartu, Estonia.

Bruns, A. (2010). News produsage in a pro-am mediasphere. In G. Meikle & G. Redden (Eds.), *News online: Transformations and continuities* (pp. 132–147). London: Palgrave.

Bruns, A. (2012). Journalists and Twitter: How Australian news organisations adapt to a new medium. *Media International Australia, 144*(1), 97–107.

Carlson, M., & Lewis, S. C. (Eds.). (2015). *Boundaries of journalism: Professionalism, practices and participation*. New York, NY: Routledge.

Cision. (2009). *George Washington University and Cision 2009 social media & online usage study*. Retrieved from http://www.gwu.edu/~newsctr/10/pdfs/gw_cision_sm_study_09.PDF.

Cremedas, M., & Lysak, S. (2011). 'New Media' skills competency of TV reporters and producers. *Electronic News, 5*(1), 41–59.

De Burgh, H. (2003). Skills are not enough: The case for journalism as an academic discipline. *Journalism, 4*(1), 95–112.

Deuze, M. (2003). The web and its journalisms: Considering the consequences of different types of news media online. *New Media and Society, 5*(2), 203–230.

Deuze, M. (2005). What is journalism? Professional identity and ideology of journalists reconsidered. *Journalism, 6*(4), 442–464.

Deuze, M., Bruns, A., & Neuberger, C. (2007). Preparing for an age of participatory news. *Journalism Practice, 1*(3), 322–338.

Diakopoulos, N., De Choudhury, M., & Naaman, M. (2012). Finding and assessing social media information sources in the context of journalism. *Proceedings of CHI'12*, Austin, Texas, USA, May 5–10.

Domingo, D., Quandt, T., Heinonen, A., Paulussen, S., Singer, J. B., & Vujnovic, M. (2008). Participatory journalism practices in the media and beyond: An international comparative study of initiatives in online newspapers. *Journalism Practice, 2*(3), 326–342.

Douglas, T. (2006, July 4). How 7/7 democratised media. *BBC*. Retrieved from http://news.bbc.co.uk/2/hi/uk_news/5142702.stm.

Evans, S. K., Pearce, K. E., Vitak, J., & Treem, J. W. (2017). Explicating affordances: A conceptual framework for understanding affordances in communication research. *Journal of Computer-Mediated Communication, 22*(1), 35–52.

Fiske, J. (1987). *Television culture*. London: Methuen & Co.

Fuchs, C., Boersma, K., Albrechtslund, A., & Sandoval, M. (Eds.). (2012). *Internet and surveillance: The challenges of web 2.0 and social media*. London: Routledge.

Gara, A. (2016, June 16). LinkedIn is the latest fast-growing tech company to give up on the stock market. *Forbes*. Retrieved from https://www.forbes.com/sites/antoinegara/2016/06/13/linkedin-is-the-latest-fast-growing-tech-company-to-give-up-on-the-stock-market/#39a073de1c9a.

García, J. A., Meier, K., Kaltenbrunner, A., Carvajal, M., & Kraus, D. (2009). Newsroom integration in Australia, Spain and Germany. *Journalism Practice, 3*(3), 1–19.

Harrison, T. M., & Brea, B. (2009). Wielding new media in Web 2.0: Exploring the history of engagement with the collaborative construction of media products. *New Media & Society, 11*(1–2), 155–178.

Heinonen, A. (2011). The journalist's relationship with users: New dimensions to conventional roles. In J. B. Singer, D. Domingo, A. Heinonen, A. Hermida, S. Paulussen, T. Quandt, et al. (Eds.), *Participatory journalism: Guarding open gates at online newspapers* (pp. 34–55). West Sussex: Wiley.

Heinrich, A. (2011). *Network journalism: Journalistic practice in interactive spheres*. Hoboken, NY: Routledge.

Hermida, A. (2010). 'Twittering' the News: The emergence of ambient journalism. *Journalism Practice, 4*(3), 297–308.

Hermida, A. (2012). Social journalism: exploring how social media is shaping journalism. In E. Siapera & A. Veglis (Eds.), *The handbook of global online journalism* (pp. 309–328). West Sussex: Wiley.

Hermida, A. (2013). #JOURNALISM: Reconfiguring journalism research about Twitter, one tweet at a time. *Digital Journalism, 1*(3), 295–313.

Hermida, A., & Thurman, N. (2008). A clash of cultures: The integration of user-generated content within professional journalistic frameworks at British Newspaper websites. *Journalism Practice, 2*(3), 343–356.

Highmore, B. (2011). *Ordinary lives: Studies in the everyday*. Oxon: Routledge.

Hirst, M., & Treadwell, G. (2011). Blogs bother me. *Journalism Practice, 5*(4), 446–461.

Hjort, M., Oskarsson, S., & Szabò, M. (2011). *A study of social media as a journalistic tool*. Report Series no. 66. Gothenburg: Department of Journalism, Media and Communication, University of Gothenburg.

Holton, A. E., & Molyneux, L. (2015). Identity lost? The personal impact of brand journalism. *Journalism*. http://doi.org/10.1177/1464884915608816.

Johnstone, J., Slawski, E., & Bowman, W. (1976). The News People: A Sociological Portrait of American Journalists and Their Work. Urbana: University of Illinois Press.

Katz, I. (2011, March 15). Andy Carvin—The man who tweeted the revolution. How an NPR strategist became the go-to source of information on Twitter during the recent uprisings in Tunisia, Egypt and Libya. *The Guardian*. Retrieved from http://www.theguardian.com/technology/2011/mar/14/andycarvin-tunisialibya-egypt-sxsw-2011.

Lasorsa, D. L., Lewis, S. C., & Holton, A. (2012). Normalizing Twitter: Journalism practice in an emerging communication space. *Journalism Studies, 13*(1), 19–36.

Lavrusik, V. (2011). How journalists are using social media to report on the Egyptian demonstrations. *Mashable*. Retrieved from http://mashable.com/2011/01/31/journalists-social-media-egypt/#6Lbj._2dD5qD.

Leonardi, P. M. (2013). Theoretical foundations for the study of sociomateriality. *Information and Organisation, 23*(2), 59–76. http://doi.org/10.1016/j.infoandorg.2013.02.002.

Lewis, S., & Westlund, O. (2015). Actors, actants, audiences, and activities in cross media news work: A matrix and a research agenda. *Digital Journalism, 3*(1), 19–37.

Livingstone, S., & Asmolov, G. (2010). Networks and the future of foreign affairs reporting. *Journalism Studies, 11*(5), 745–760.

Lynley, M. (2011, May 22). Murdoch says $580 million Myspace buy a huge mistake. *Business Insider*. Retrieved from https://www.businessinsider.com.au/murdoch-says-580-million-myspace-buy-a-huge-mistake-2011-10.

Marwick, A. E., & boyd, d. (2011). I tweet honestly, I tweet passionately: Twitter users, context collapse, and the imagined audience. *New Media & Society, 13*(1), 114–133.

Messner, M., Linke, M., & Eford, A. (2012). Shoveling tweets: An analysis of the microblogging engagement of traditional news organisations. *ISOJ Journal, 2*(1), 76–90.

Mitchelstein, E., & Boczkowski, P. J. (2009). Between tradition and change: A review of recent research on online news production. *Journalism, 10*(5), 562–586.

Newman, N. (2009). The rise of social media and its impact on mainstream journalism: A study of how newspapers and broadcasters in the UK and US are responding to a wave of participatory social media, and a historic shift in control towards individual consumers. *Reuters Institute for the Study of Journalism*. Retrieved from https://reutersinstitute.politics.ox.ac.uk/sites/

default/files/The%20rise%20%20social%20media%20and%20its%20impact%20on%20mainstream%20journalism_0.pdf.

O'Sullivan, J., & Heinonen, A. (2008). Old values, new media: Journalism role perceptions in a changing world. *Journalism Practice, 2*(3), 357–371.

Parr, B. (2009, May 26). The New York Times hires a social media editor: Does it need one? *Mashable*. Retrieved from http://mashable.com/2009/05/26/nyt-social-media-editor/.

Posetti, J. (2009). Transforming journalism…140 characters at a time. *Rhodes Journalism Review, 29*, 38–40.

Posetti, J., & Lo, P. (2012). The Twitterisation of ABC's emergency and disaster communication. *The Australian Journal of Emergency Management, 27*(1), 34.

Revers, M. (2014). Journalistic professionalism as performance and boundary work: Source relations at the state house. *Journalism, 15*(1), 37–52.

Sacco, V., & Bossio, D. (2017). Don't tweet this! How journalists and media organisations negotiate tensions emerging from the implementation of social media policy in newsrooms. *Digital Journalism, 5*(2), 177–193.

Saltzis, K., & Dickinson, R. (2008). Inside the changing newsroom: Journalists' responses to media convergence. *Aslib Proceedings, 60*(3), 216–228.

Sheffer, M. L., & Schultz, B. (2009). Are blogs changing the news values of newspaper reporters? *Web Journal of Mass Communication Research, 16*. Retrieved from http://wjmcr.org/vol16.

Standley, T. C. (2013). Traditional news media's use of social media. In A. Albarran (Ed.), *The social media industries* (pp. 132–145). New York: Routledge.

Tsukayama, H. (2016, February 11). The death of Twitter as we know it. *The Washington Post*. Retrieved from https://www.washingtonpost.com/news/the-switch/wp/2016/02/11/the-death-of-twitter-as-we-know-it/.

Usher, N. (2014). *Making news at the New York Times*. Ann Arbor: University of Michigan Press.

van Dijk, J. (2013). *The culture of connectivity: A critical history of social media*. Oxford: Oxford University Press.

Williams, R. (1958). Culture is ordinary. In R. Williams & R. Gable (Eds.), *Resources of hope: Culture, democracy, socialism (1987)*. (pp. 3–14). London: Verso.

CHAPTER 2

Social Media and Journalism Practice

In January 2016, the online aggregator and news site, *The Huffington Post*, announced that it would be adding a disclaimer to all election reportage about the Republican presidential nominee, Donald Trump. Every time a reader clicked on a *Huffington Post* article about Trump, they would find the following message: 'Note to our readers: Donald Trump is a serial liar, rampant xenophobe, racist, misogynist, birther and bully who has repeatedly pledged to ban all Muslims—1.6 billion members of an entire religion—from entering the U.S.' (Sterne 2016). Each of the claims was linked to *Huffington Post* reports that evidenced Trump's transgressions. Not only is it unusual for a news organisation to use such overtly subjective language to describe a presidential nominee, it is also a significant change from the relative objectivity expected of contemporary political journalism. For *The Huffington Post*, one of the most popular political sites in the world and the first digital news site to win a Pulitzer Prize (Calderone 2012), this lack of political objectivity would once have been a jarring reminder of the online aggregator's lack of journalistic sophistication. So how is it possible that one of the bedrocks of traditional journalism—the practice of objectivity in reportage—could be so blatantly pushed aside? Some of this oppositional reportage was certainly influenced by the strategic positioning of media outlets competing for attention during an increasingly partisan presidential election—and even the discursive style of Donald Trump himself. But these strategic and political tactics are only one part of the explanation; the apparent acceptability of such overt subjectivity

D. Bossio, *Journalism and Social Media*,
DOI 10.1007/978-3-319-65472-0_2

in the reportage of the presidential election is also framed by the culture of communication on social media, which has created opportunities to disrupt seemingly inviolable norms of reportage.

This chapter explores the transitions occurring in some traditional norms of journalistic practice: maintaining objectivity in reportage, using processes of verification and, finally, asserting professional autonomy over individual work practice. Norms of practice can be defined as the behaviours continually represented as the ideal standard for professional journalism. For example, maintaining 'objectivity' in journalism practice is framed by belief in journalism's social role to inform the public without partisanship. Thus, norms of practice are also ideological, allowing journalists and news organisations to claim jurisdiction over a particular body of knowledge and practice (Lewis 2012, p. 840). While this chapter explores the representation of 'ideal' norms of practice, it does so with implicit acknowledgement that 'actual' practices are very much influenced by a confluence of organisational, technological and other factors.

This chapter will argue that norms of journalism practice have transitioned in response to the social and technological affordances enabled by increasing use of social media. This has allowed traditional norms of objectivity, verification and professional autonomy to transition into new forms of journalistic practice that are increasingly collaborative and prioritise authentic and transparent processes of presenting the news. Some of these innovations in everyday journalistic practice include the potential for collaboration with online sources, the immediate and global distribution of source materials, and the prioritisation of an 'authentic' authorial voice. It seems that journalists who are using these new practices have been influenced by social media cultures that prioritise sharing, authentic self-expression and the rejection of notions of a universal truth. However, the transition of professional journalistic practice to social media environments has also challenged legacy news organisations and the overall constitution of journalism as a professional institution. Indeed, these new forms of practice suggest that the biggest change in journalistic practice is actually the broader institutional understanding of journalism itself—from an autonomous authority to an important, but nonetheless collaborative stakeholder in creating the news.

To explore these changes, this chapter utilises a historical and social framework to trace the transition from traditional to social media-enabled norms of practice. These changes are contextualised as part of a number of interconnected changes occurring at the level of the journalistic practitioner, as well as news organisations and the institution of journalism itself. As suggested in the introduction to this book, while the focus on journalistic practice is important, it is only one aspect of the complex changes occurring in journalism due to increasing use of online and social media technologies. Instead, this chapter shows that journalistic practice is in a state of transition, with a number of different professional interests, organisational policies, professional norms and social, cultural and political environments shaping the ways journalists are able to practise. While it would be impossible to outline every single influence on individual journalistic practice, this chapter will illustrate the way three dominant, traditional professional practices have been actively mediated and negotiated by journalists in the midst of a profession in transition.

Journalism Norms of Practice: An Historical Context

Though many journalists have integrated social media into everyday practices, there remains scepticism about whether the quality and veracity of information found on social media platforms could ever equate to traditional reporting practices. Journalists often appear to rely on established norms of practice to produce news, simply transferring traditional journalism practices to new communication tools (Singer 2005; Hermida 2012). In the short term, it makes sense that journalists would view social media through the same conceptual lens as other communication tools, and work according to the established practices through which they define their professional status. However, as Paulussen (2016) suggests, the accumulation of these changes over time shows that the evolution of journalism is actually quite dynamic, incorporating new individual practices, new organisational strategies and new understandings of journalism as an institution.

If we take a long-term, historical view of journalistic practice, we see that seemingly indispensable norms of journalism practice, such as objectivity, verification and professional autonomy, are not only socially and culturally constructed, but have also been continually negotiated over time. The industrialisation of news—that is, the payment of people to find and report on news events—has a relatively short history of about 200 years (Schudson 2011, p. 64) linked to the technological development of fast printing presses and the social development of increased literacy, especially amongst middle-class populations. For example, the first newspapers in Australia in the early 1800s simply printed governmental notices to the colonies and four-month-old news from England that arrived via convict and supply ships (Walker 1976). However, two important social and cultural changes occurred as a result of increased printed news production and distribution. Firstly, at an organisational level, publishers began to pay journalists to write news, and to consider the production values and popularity of their content against other newspapers. Secondly, at a broader cultural and social level, the wide readership of newspapers created a sense of a 'reachable' public that shared a community sentiment, morals and social and cultural norms. Benedict Anderson (1983) famously conceptualised newspaper readership as an 'imagined community'. Describing reading the newspaper as a kind of 'morning prayer', the reader believes that 'the ceremony he performs is being replicated simultaneously by thousands of others of whose existence he is confident, yet of whose identity he has not the slightest notion' (Anderson 1983, p. 46). The creation of a community around the distribution of news created a sense of shared culture and knowledge. It is these two social and industrial changes in the development of newspapers that also created a foundation for commercial and professional development of journalistic practice.

The first real push towards professionalised journalistic practice did not come until after the 1920s. Indeed, early newspaper and journalism history is marked by editorial partisanship, commercial and government influence and sensational news content. Early newspapers created gossip and colour stories, mixed with copious advertising and political news (Schudson 2011, p. 65). The development of the 'penny press', the telegraph and their associated shorter writing styles improved the distribution of news, but not the partisanship of the content. The number of paid journalists also increased as better printing technologies allowed the small press to flourish, but the reputation of these 'correspondents' was never complementary to the trade. Despite this, the popularity of news content meant that journalists had become a large and distinct occupational group, and soon demanded better pay and public image. Thus, the emergence of journalism as a profession began, coupled with the rise of professional associations and a focus on ethical codes of practice and training that determined more precisely the boundaries of journalism's professional role.

After the First and Second World Wars, a strong social belief in the scientific method also began to emerge, expressed as the prioritisation of objectivity, professional autonomy and verification in journalism.

Schudson (1978, p. 141) suggests that while verification and neutrality promoted use of 'straight facts', objectivity was seen as an important journalistic method in a post-war society weary of pro-government reportage. These practices offered a way to gain critical distance and regain the audience's trust in the seriousness of journalism. These seemingly 'scientific' modes of practice became what Lippmann (1920) called the 'cardinal' part of training professional journalists. Coupled with the increasing professionalisation of news came a broader social reliance on professional media-makers and journalists to decide on, and represent, the news of the day. Even when objectivity was attacked in the 1960s and 1970s as a refusal to critique the traditional structures of power in society (Schudson 1978, p. 160), it remained one of the most important tenets of the increasingly investigative and specialised reporting practices of journalists. News was, and continues to be, decided on, produced and disseminated by professional workers in complex, hierarchical and commercialised organisations, using norms of practice that have been routinised and institutionalised (Tuchman 1978).

Simons (2007, p. 245) refers to the strength of these institutional norms and behaviours when she describes the 'religiosity' with which journalists understand their profession. These core practices have been ascribed this religiosity through continual enactment of 'rituals' of practice (Schudson 1978, p. 192) in journalism education and training, newsroom organisation and representation in various media. The adherence to professional norms and ideologies has even been characterised as a kind of journalistic personality trait; for many years, journalism education and employability guides described journalists as having an inherent 'news sense' that enables them to understand and decide what should be considered news (Vocational Guidance Bureau 1964). It is therefore understandable that, in this context, journalists and news organisations have not easily adapted to the changes brought to journalistic practice by adoption of online and social media, and that newsroom culture has been found to be 'marked by reactive, defensive and pragmatic traits' in regard to changes wrought by social media (Boczkowski 2004, p. 51). However, as journalism transitions into digital, online and social media-enabled environments, small changes and negotiations have eventually contributed to significant shifts within the industry and to journalism practice (Küng 2015). Nowhere is this more evident than in changes to journalistic use of objectivity.

From Objectivity to Authenticity

Objectivity is one of the defining norms of professional practice in journalism. It frames a number of behaviours and practices, such as detachment and non-partisanship in reportage, attempted balance in finding news sources, and a distinct style of news writing (Mindich 1998, p. 2). Norms like objectivity are important for a number of reasons. Firstly, they encourage group identification through the articulation of a professional self-identity (Durkheim and Lukes 2014). Through this professional self-identity, norms of practice identify the boundaries of a profession, setting it apart from other professions, as well as amateur practice (see Emery and Emery 1996). Finally, norms of practice register a kind of self-discipline that can be organisationally practised and used to admit new members to the profession—or keep them out. Objectivity is thus expressed as an inviolable tenet of journalism's professional ethics, journalism education and occupational routines—and is strongly defended against challenge (Tuchman 1972, p. 660). For example, when news blogs and bloggers began to gain popularity with new online readerships in the early 2000s, some journalists dismissed this form of news as the 'cult of the amateur', referring to traditional norms of practice to create the boundaries for professional practice—and to keep bloggers 'out' of the profession.

Perhaps some journalists reacted defensively to the introduction of blogging as a new format for news reportage because it fostered practices that so effectively challenged traditional norms of practice. The practices that have emerged from online media production are based on their technological determinants for increased accessibility and participation of audiences in media production and dissemination. These new technological frameworks have centred on audiences' ability to produce, distribute and share these new media forms such as review sites, commenting systems, photo and video sharing, blogging and microblogging (Mandiberg 2012, p. 1). However, these technical affordances have also influenced changes in communications practices, which prioritise sharing of new media forms and cutting out the journalistic 'middle man' by directly engaging with specific content and users. The ability to engage with, and share, content, especially personal news and information, has subsequently led to the emergence of particular social media cultures, based on the articulation of an authentic representation of self-identity, as well as an authentic engagement with 'followers' of these online representations.

'Authenticity' is defined as a mode of representational practice that emerged out of blogging culture, describing how online content could be represented as an extension of a blogger's 'real self': a means of self-expression and exploration (Reed 2005, p. 236). Though this mode of self-representation is not confined to online and social media (Giddens 1991), a culture of sharing on social media has meant that 'being authentic' has become an important aspect of online self-actualisation and representation of media content. Marwick and boyd (2011) found that by representing themselves online, some content producers saw social media as an intimate space, with an imagined audience reinforcing social connections. Others saw the audience as 'themselves' and derided creating content for a particular audience as inauthentic self-commoditisation (Marwick and boyd 2011, p. 120). Instead, modes of authenticity were deemed important as representations of 'real' social interactions in the online space. Similarly, interactions were based on attracting followers of content, rather than 'fans' (Marwick and boyd 2011). This eschews the sense of elite social authority that traditional norms of journalism practice might otherwise promote (Abidin 2016, p. 2). While practices of authenticity and objectivity are not necessarily opposed as techniques for representing news, it is the implied social distance that traditional norms of objectivity seemingly promote that is challenged by social media representations of news. Thus, new practices that prioritise authenticity in reportage have shown the limits of objectivity as an ideal norm of journalistic practice.

For example, the changing coverage of global climate change has shown the limits of objectivity as a norm of reportage. While the global scientific consensus is that human activity has contributed to global warming, and that this will lead to significant issues arising from climate change in the future, initial journalistic insistence on 'objectivity', especially in reporting the views of 'climate sceptics', has been criticised. While the journalistic norms of objectivity and balance would dictate that an oppositional viewpoint be covered in reportage of a news event, the attention given to climate sceptics has been criticised as undermining the validity of the consequences of climate change (Boykoff and Boykoff 2007). John Oliver, a comedian who uses satire of news events on his television programme *Last Week Tonight*, created a humorous critique of mainstream media's use of norms of objectivity in a 'statistically representative climate change debate' (Last Week Tonight 2014). The resulting 'debate', with one climate change sceptic debating with 100 climate change scientists, illustrated that reportage of climate science as a 'debate' instead of a fact was misleading to the public. Other critiques of enforced journalistic 'balance' led to some news organisational change in reportage of climate change. *The New York Times* no longer publishes letters from climate change deniers and the *BBC* has refused to give broadcast attention to climate change denial (Hiltzik 2015).

Challenges to traditional norms of practice, as well as increasing social media engagement by some journalists, have developed into opportunities to present more authentic forms of presenting news online and on social media. The most obvious change is the increasing prioritisation of the social or personal aspect of news stories posted on social media, as well as engaging directly with followers by responding to queries, posting links to other sources and asking the audience questions about stories. Another important part of this change is increasing use of affect and emotion, rather than objectivity or neutrality, as a way to ensure a more authentic engagement with audiences (Russell 2016). While emotion has always been part of journalism (Wahl-Jorgensen 2013), online and social media communication cultures allow much more for emotional or political positioning of news content. A recent example of this shift is the positioning of the journalist in the popular podcast series, *Serial*. The podcast launched in 2014 as a spin-off to the popular podcast series, *This American Life*, and almost immediately broke download records. The series follows producer Sarah Koenig's investigation of the murder of teenager Hae Min Lee and whether the convicted murderer, Adnan Syed, was actually innocent of the crime. This deceptively simple premise is produced with a mix of high-quality, 'television drama' style episodic storytelling, as well as 'authentic' emotional appeals that serve to involve the audience in the investigation. The language of the podcast is intimate and conversational in tone: it 'sounds like your smart friend is investigating a murder and telling you about it' (Larson 2014). Indeed, the producers—who never describe themselves as journalists—did not complete the investigation of the murder before editing the episodes together.

Whereas a traditional journalistic investigation would generally compile all the evidence and interviews needed to make a decisive representation of the facts, *Serial* allows the producers and the audience to participate in the investigation together, sharing the drama of new discoveries and continually debating theories about Syed's guilt or innocence. The investigation is never actually conclusive, and while that would often mean failure in traditional journalism, in *Serial* this is celebrated—and promoted—as testimony to the audience's intimate relationship with both the subject matter and the producers themselves. This is seen from the first episode of *Serial*, in which the host, Ira Glass, describes the producers as having 'flipped back and forth, over and over, in their thinking about whether Adnan committed the murder. And when you listen to the series, you experience those flips with them' (Koenig 2014). The positioning and tone of the *Serial* investigation and its reportage illustrates the way forms of authenticity are making their way into journalistic work. These developments in journalistic practice, popularised by online and social media use of emotion, intimacy and modes of authenticity in representations of news, have also influenced long-institutionalised modes of professional journalism.

While *Serial* is an example of how some journalists have embraced modes of authenticity in reportage, this has generally also been tempered by more traditional boundaries around what constitutes professional practice (Lasorsa et al. 2012). Representation of self in online environments is mediated by understanding and engagement with an 'imagined audience'. However, journalists are also mediating the space between personal and commercial modes of authenticity, as well as creating content for a particular professional identification. For example, recent academic research has traced the more commercially viable aspects of this 'authenticity' on social media platforms, where social media 'influencers' cultivate large audience retention and engagement through the representation of their personal lives. They often seek to monetise this engagement through commercial agreements that are used to promote products in 'everyday life' (Abidin 2015). Some social media influencers represent themselves through an everyday persona or give the impression of candid, behind the scenes access to their lives (Marwick 2015, p. 139), creating a sense of closeness or 'intimacy' with their online community. Abidin (2015) separates ideas of intimacy and authenticity because in the commercial space of social media influence, it is possible for influencers to be motivated by commerce—and for followers to be aware of this—as long as there is a sense of intimacy shared between them. This sense of intimacy and authenticity is a little more complicated in the professional space, where online and offline work cultures are brought together. For example, Gregg (2011, p. 3) suggests that bringing contemporary work cultures online has created a 'presence bleed', in which boundaries between the professional and personal must be renegotiated. The techniques used in commercial branding are now being employed in both personal and professional use of social media to increase followers and online popularity (Marwick 2013). Thus, Hedman and Djerf-Pierre (2013, p. 372) suggest that while journalists' 'authentic' use of social media can be seen as part of an increasing audience engagement, it could also be seen as opportunistic; a component of personal career-building or the corporate branding of news organisations. Journalists might actually be responding to organisational pressure to represent themselves as a media 'brand', especially if their follower numbers might benefit their news organisation (Tandoc and Vos 2016). Similarly, Holton and Molyneux (2015) suggest that journalists 'feel pressure to stake a claim on their beat, develop a presence as an expert and act as a representative of the news organisation'.

This suggests that for a journalist attempting to use social media in their practice, there are competing priorities and demands in organisational and institutional contexts that complicate representation of professional work. While these modes of authenticity have been used in a number of complex ways, including for professional and commercial benefit, they point to the new interconnections between audience need, technological change, organisational structures and institutional norms that affect journalistic practice in a social media age. Most importantly, however, some journalistic practice has begun to incorporate a patchwork of journalistic endeavour, curatorial effort and collaborative construction. Without the expectation of objectivity in the news, some journalists are now using a number of other approaches to assert their public credibility—most notably, use of so-called 'transparent' reporting practices.

From Verification to Transparency

The first principle of ethical journalistic practice espoused by the Australian Journalism Code of Ethics is: 'Report and interpret honestly, striving for accuracy, fairness and disclosure of all essential facts. Do not suppress relevant available facts, or give distorting emphasis.' According to this code, journalists should, above all else, strive for honesty and accuracy; traditional journalistic practices sustain this through processes of verification. Verification and objectivity are linked as central aspects of journalistic professional practice; where objectivity asserts the credibility of the journalist, practices of verification assert the credibility of journalistic content. There are no standard practices that make up a 'scientific method' of verification; rather, journalists adhere to an abstract ethical commitment to truth and accuracy that makes up an important part of their professional self-identity.

In the post-war period, the focus on investigative processes of journalism elevated truth-telling to the realm of 'god term' (Zelizer 2004), where a verifiable notion of truth, devoid of influence or patronage, could seemingly be excavated from falsehood through the professional practices enshrined in journalism. These truths would then be delivered to the public as journalism's most important service to democratic function. This type of journalistic practice represented truth as a unitary 'thing to be found' by the journalist—an objective, verifiable version of the news that would be the sole understanding of the event. This kind of 'truth seeking' has been an enduring norm of journalistic practice, despite the sustained academic criticism of the epistemological concept of a 'stable' notion of truth (Zelizer 2004). Theorists such as Derrida (see Caputo 1997) and Foucault (1980) questioned the notion of a universally understood or 'knowable' truth, in favour of the subjective representations and politicised relations that create dominant discourses. Nonetheless, verification and accuracy have persisted as professional norms, requiring a journalist's commitment to finding 'a kind of "pure" accuracy (literal truth), an accuracy of what is told (uncritical reliance on an attributed source), a larger accuracy (concerning a story's overall thrust in context), and accuracy of interpretation' (Shapiro et al. 2013). Thus, verification defines an 'essential nature' both of contemporary journalism, expressed through a methodological commitment to accurate truth-telling, and to notions of truth itself (Shapiro et al. 2013). By determining a universal truth in news events, journalists continually assert their jurisdiction over the definition of news and its meaning; thus, verification is both a self-disciplining and self-defining practice.

Verification has been central to the understanding of ethical journalism but new voices in online and social media have challenged the representation of universal truth in the news—and the centrality of the journalist in presenting it. Importantly, the prioritisation of authentic self-expression on social media does not mean that representations of news do not adhere to particular standards of practice. Indeed, even the early emergence of citizen journalism blog sites like *OhMyNews* in South Korea and independent news websites like *Crikey* in Australia showed strong commitment to standards of ethical and professional online news reporting. While traditional journalistic norms of objectivity and universal truth were positioned as the ideal of more elitist, broadcast-style practice, early online news reportage instead prioritised transparency and inclusion of audiences in the news reporting process as a more authentic way of demonstrating how an online journalist arrived at a particular 'truth'. Importantly, this representation of news was necessarily unfinished and subject to the additional commentary and fact-checking of interested audiences. Of course, just like traditional journalism, transparency is an ideal of online journalism and not always adhered to by bloggers and citizen journalists in reality. Nonetheless, processes of transparency have become an increasingly important part of engaging with social media news audiences.

The increasing use of social media has presented both opportunity and challenge to traditional processes of verification used by journalists. On the one hand, quick access to sources, short video and eyewitness content has made it easier than ever before for journalists to verify news reports. On the other hand, instantaneous publishing and the viral effects of popular social media content have meant that false and hoax news have become ever-growing problems for journalists. Accessing other forms of news and representations of truth also creates an institutional challenge for journalism—even when news is 'fake', or partisan, audiences do not always rely on the social authority of journalists to point this out. In this context, some journalists have considered it important to exhibit how and why their news stories should be seen as credible. Processes of transparency have been referred to as a kind of ethical salve to criticism of mainstream news reportage as elitist, homogeneous and scandal-driven (Karlsson 2008).

Transparency thus relates to the openness of both the journalist and the news product to scrutiny from audiences. This might come in the form of presenting or explaining the processes of news source selection, or justification for the particular representation of a news event. Journalists have practised this transparency by publishing links to source materials, publishing entire interviews, or even creating separate websites dedicated to publishing extra materials and 'behind the scenes' discussion of larger news stories. This kind of transparent practice was used in the production of 'Curious Chicago', an experimental news-making project supported by *WBEZ* public radio. The project is run through *Tumblr*, where interested locals post questions about Chicago.

The platform essentially allows audience members some control over editorial processes, as well as some participation in the creation of a story. Journalists demonstrate their processes of investigating a story, inviting discussion, correction and additional information. The results of the investigations are then broadcast on a weekly programme and published on a website. This practice of transparency also has an effect on the news reports themselves—the tone of reportage is intimate, playful and immediate, putting the spotlight on those reporting what was happening to them, rather than on journalists, as the centre of knowledge.

The importance of transparency has been central to contemporary debate by journalists about ethical practice; for some, transparency is a new mode of accountability that replaces the critical distance of objectivity (Vos and Craft 2016). For others, transparency is a naïve form of deference to the audience that results in obfuscation of important information (Cunningham 2006). While transparency has been prioritised as a form of openness and accountability in the decisions and relationships that produce reportage, the affordances that have emerged from social media platforms have situated transparency slightly differently as 'making visible'—engaging with audiences during or after the publication of a news story through source material and social interactions (Chadha and Koliska 2015, p. 216). While this approach still prioritises the public role of the journalist in a functioning democracy, it does so by asserting this role as part of a community of interested stakeholders, rather than an unquestioned expert. This mode of practice focusses on the individual audience members as part of a conversation—some have expertise, some are interested observers and some are merely finding the conversation as part of their daily news diet, but all are part of news dialogue. Despite the fact that transparent processes do not require input from the audience in principle, the popularity of social media engagement has fostered participatory forms of transparency. These have included more opportunities for interested audiences to discuss and challenge particular representations of news, or to participate in creating the news story itself. This 'transparent' approach to journalism and media production means that audiences are now engaged in the traditional backstage creation and 'sewing together' of news events. Rather than simply having access to the news as a finished product, transparent journalistic practices engage interested stakeholders in the news event by sourcing, verifying and discussing what should be incorporated into a representation of news. This is the key to transparency in new modes of journalistic practice using social media: the understanding of news and information as necessarily iterative, to be corrected and updated as new evidence and knowledge come to light. This is also an institutional shift in the constitution of journalistic social authority; the construction of news is seen as a collaborative effort facilitated by a professional journalist, rather than the sole decision of a trusted—and unquestioned—media authority.

These reporting practices suggest some of the institutional changes that have come alongside the individual practice and organisational changes in journalism, especially the more active and dominant role given to various publics on social media (Russell 2016). In this environment, journalists are becoming more cognizant of how social media cultures differ in expectation of engagement with the audience. It has become more acceptable for a journalist not to report news as a 'finished product' because the immediacy of web content allows for constant addition to, and correction of, stories posted online. This has nonetheless also created some issues about the veracity of information posted on social media. Some news organisations have baulked at any large-scale participatory production processes in the newsroom due to the number of falsified documents, images and eyewitness accounts posted and shared through social media. Larger media organisations, especially those that utilise user-generated content, have used a variety of tools to verify social media content. For example, the *BBC's* Verification Hub sifts through about 3000 user-generated contributions sent to the *BBC* (Turner 2012) or posted on social media every day. Approximately 20 staff use a number of tools to verify content, including talking to journalists in the field, cross-checking other social media reports, using photo metadata or triangulating locations to verify information provided to them. They will also use search terms to see what is trending on *Twitter*, and whether the material is being discussed by their own contacts. Perhaps the most interesting verification technique used by journalists at the hub is simply contacting whoever posted the material—the staff suggested that a traditional interview with an informant can often help the journalist find out more about the material and whether the source is credible (Turner 2012). These issues and negotiations are nonetheless productive tensions—they demand the development of better traditional practices and new innovations in response to changing modes of communication. While the number of voices on social media has meant that an objective representation of a single truth is no longer expected or viable, the increased possibility of false news warrants immediate and public censure of unprofessional conduct. What constitutes professional conduct, however, is also changing in social media environments and journalists are using new forms of verification—alongside traditional forms of journalism—to ensure their credibility to an increasingly discerning and empowered audience. In this way, transparency also relates to accountability; engaging in online communities and showing the process of reportage can be seen as a new ethical ideal in a networked social media environment.

From Professional Autonomy to Collaboration

Contemporary journalism is represented as a privileged role, because a journalist is able to independently and autonomously decide what information makes up their reportage of a news event. Journalism makes its institutional claim to professional status through its autonomous jurisdiction over the selection and prioritisation of news events. While journalists commit to not prioritising their own views in reportage by practising objectivity, they nonetheless choose the context, sources and mode of representation of events. It is through this autonomy that journalists claim their professional knowledge and authority. By the late 1950s, accountability was also an indicator of a journalist's social and cultural power—journalists were represented as 'gatekeepers' for the public; they decided what the public needed to know and how they should know it (Domingo et al. 2008, p. 326). In asserting this authority, the individual journalist was represented as being responsible for 'selecting, writing, editing, positioning, scheduling, repeating and otherwise massaging information to become news' (Shoemaker et al. 2009, p. 74). In reality, news production is the collective effort of the newsroom, with individual expertise utilised, but also shaped by norms of practice and organisational routines. However, ideals of journalistic practice prioritise representation of the journalist as the gatekeeper autonomously controlling whether information is important enough to be communicated as news.

While independence and autonomy are important markers of professional practice, they are also an important part of the 'boundary keeping' (Lewis 2012) that ensures no encroachment on the social and cultural power journalists enjoy. The right to control what the public understands as news assumes autonomous power, even if it is expressed as a public service or gatekeeping role. However, as we have seen, social media prioritises public participation, and audiences are more involved in the process of creating, shaping, and sharing information about events they witness (Hermida 2012). Interested audience members even become users and co-producers in news by participating in collaborative processes of making or sharing news (Heinonen 2011). Thus, in the context of asserting autonomy, journalistic practices have been seen to shift in social media environments, accommodating and negotiating the views and input from engaged news audiences. Singer (2007, p. 79) suggests that the move to online and social media-enabled news environments has not devalued the professional practice of autonomy; rather, the expression of autonomy has shifted from a focus on external modes of power to a critique of all expressions of social and cultural power, including journalism. This critique has emerged through the successful use of collaborative reportage practices to create shared, collective knowledge and ideas (Singer 2005). These collaborative forms of news illustrate that contemporary journalism can comprise the collective decisions of those affected by news, rather than one autonomous individual or news organisation. Journalists become less autonomous, but more curatorial in their approach, interweaving different eyewitness statements and translating news narratives into a coherent shape and context for their particular readership.

A more curatorial approach by journalists means that news is constantly re-articulated through the addition, re-interpretation and correction of information. Subsequent to this change is the broader shift in the professional authority of journalists; there is no longer one autonomous, ethical, professional approach to news production in this environment. Instead, journalists and audiences are collaborators, who also share oversight and correction of professional behaviour (Singer 2007, p. 79). Collaborative practice also means that boundaries of professional/non-professional practice become blurred; focus is instead diverted to how particular news events foster relations between different media producers and publics invested in news production, witnessing, interpreting and disputing common news narratives. Thus, collaborative journalism practices increase possibilities for more diverse, open and transparent forms of journalism online.

A good example of this is *Al Jazeera's Sharek* network, which facilitates the use and distribution of user-generated content through an accreditation system. Content on *Sharek* is available in several languages and in regions from which it is difficult to report. *Al Jazeera*'s journalists work to moderate and distribute content submitted from social media through its online portal. Regular and reliable contributors are accredited and trained, and their content is made available on the *Sharek* website without moderation. Accredited citizen journalists are also able to apply for journalism training, and their content is more likely to make it on to the *Al Jazeera* network. *Al Jazeera*'s head of social media, Riyaad Minty, said the network's comprehensive coverage of the Arab Spring was made possible due to the collaborative nature of reportage during the event; much of the network's imagery and video came from citizens and activists, many of whom were credited in official reports (Bartlett 2012). While the incorporation of *Sharek* content into *Al Jazeera* shows organisational willingness to foster collaboration, this is tempered by strict editorial controls over how and when the content is utilised by journalists. Thus, the transition from autonomy to collaborative journalistic processes cannot necessarily be seen as relinquishing overall control of the editorial process; so far, it is a more complex transition of the social role of the journalist from the sole gatekeeper of truth to a collaborative facilitator of public dialogue.

The inherent complexity of collaborative approaches to news-making is most obvious when journalists lose control of their facilitation of the news narrative. For example, the reportage of Irish Australian Jill Meagher's rape and murder in 2012 horrified Australians and galvanised many into political action. Thousands gathered in the suburb where she was abducted, marching in support of Meagher's grieving family, but also in protest against violent behaviour towards women (Zielinski 2013). However, the arrest of a suspect in Meagher's murder was increasingly problematised by the intense social media interest and discussion of her disappearance (Lowe 2012). Jill Meagher was mentioned almost every 11 seconds on *Facebook* and *Twitter* once news of the arrest was confirmed. Despite public pleas from the police, Meagher's husband and family, and even some sections of traditional mainstream media, social media hatred sites directed at Meagher's accused killer published images of his face and details of his private life. Media law experts warned that comments posted on blogs or social media could be subject to defamation or contempt of court proceedings, and could jeopardise the prosecution of the case. The social media buzz around the case became so prominent that the magistrate hearing the case made the unprecedented move of banning all publication of information, apart from the accused's image, from all media, including social media (Lowe 2012). What this example shows is that the speed, intimacy and easy dissemination of content creates both challenges and opportunities for collaboration practices using social media.

The disruption that social media discussion of news events can create is perhaps indicative of why journalists and news organisations have been so hesitant to innovate practices that do not fit standardised and institutionalised news routines (Domingo 2008). Indeed, change to journalism practice appears to be slow, reactive and often far from innovative due to perceived risks. However, issues in journalism practice such as lack of verification, the 'media pack' mentality and creating sensationalist or exploitative news content are not new issues in journalism practice. The growth of social media use in news means that these types of issues now have instantaneous and global audience reach. Utilising the benefits of the social media community without compromising the quality of journalism is possible—and some innovative journalists are adapting traditional modes of journalistic practice to do so. The journalists and media organisations that have benefitted from shifts in traditional production practices have continued to recognise the importance of journalistic expertise, but this is foregrounded as a mode of public engagement to create increased value for the community it serves. That is, professional journalism utilises social media to foster connection to communities and these connections are best maintained when journalists, sources and interested stakeholders in the news are working together, not so much to create a unified representation of truth, but to create conversation. While conversation is not constitutive of journalism's social importance, it is the societal actions that stem from these conversations, whether in the form of activism, public outcry or other forms of political and cultural change, that illustrate journalism's social value. Traditional journalism once brought the information to create those social changes; now, journalists and audiences create that information together. Thus, the biggest change in journalistic practice is not so much the practices themselves, but the broader institutional authority of the journalist.

Conclusion

In this chapter, changes to journalistic practice have been explored through transitions in three seemingly sacrosanct processes of reportage: objectivity, verification and professional autonomy. While the historical context for the development of these practices shows that they are arguably new to journalism, they have nonetheless become entrenched in the description of individual, organisational and institutional cultures of journalism. Processes of objectivity, verification and professional autonomy are as much a part of the professional self-identity and social authority of journalism as they are ideals of practice. While it is arguable whether these ideals of practice are actually achievable in the reality of everyday journalism, they can be considered 'strategic rituals' of journalism (Tuchman 1978), represented as the essential characteristics of good journalism practice, and defended as the markers of journalism's social and cultural authority.

This chapter has shown how objectivity, verification and professional autonomy are transitioning to incorporate practices of authenticity, transparency and collaboration. Examples in this chapter show that particular social media cultures prioritising openness and collaboration with audiences are being adopted by journalists and challenging the way traditional practices are valued in this space. This is not to say that professional journalists are being left behind by the changes to journalistic practice. Indeed, some professional journalists have been at the forefront of innovation in traditional journalistic practices within social media environments, or have been key actors in 'normalising' new processes, negotiating their use to fit into particular organisational or institutional norms of practice. Many of the issues faced by journalists using social media in their practice are necessarily productive; they highlight how journalism, like all communication practices, must respond to technological changes, as well as the social and cultural changes that emerge alongside them. Thus, it is not necessarily the expertise or skill of the journalist that is being renegotiated in social media environments, nor the need for professional journalism overall. Rather, the transition in journalistic practices is due to the changing relations between journalists and their audiences and, thus, their changing role in social life. Indeed, it is impossible to understand journalism and social media without understanding the processes of collaboration, engagement and sharing that now mark journalism and audience relations. The next chapter thus focusses on the relationship between journalists and audiences on social media.

References

Abidin, C. (2015). Communicative intimacies: Influencers and perceived interconnectedness. *ADA: A Journal of Gender, New Media and Technology, 8*. Retrieved from http://adanewmedia.org/2015/11/issue8-abidin/.

Abidin, C. (2016). Visibility labour: Engaging with influencers' fashion brands and #OOTD advertorial campaigns on Instagram. *Media International Australia, 161*(1), 86–100.

Anderson, B. (1983). *Imagined communities: Reflections on the origin and spread of nationalism*. London: Verso.
Bartlett, R. (2012, May 4). Al Jazeera to relaunch citizen media platform Sharek. *Journalism.co.uk*. Retrieved from https://www.journalism.co.uk/news/al-jazeera-to-launch-new-multilingual-citizen-media-platform/s2/a549099/.
Boczkowski, P. (2004). *Digitizing the news: Innovation in online newspapers*. Cambridge, MA: The MIT Press.
Boykoff, M. T., & Boykoff, J. M. (2007). Climate change and journalistic norms: A case-study of US mass-media coverage. *Geoforum, 38*(6), 1190–1204. 10.1016/j.geoforum.2007.01.008.YKOFF.
Calderone, M. (2012, April 17). Huffington Post wins Pulitzer Prize. *Huffington Post*. Retrieved from http://www.huffingtonpost.com.au/entry/huffington-post-pulitzer-prize-2012_n_1429169.
Caputo, J. (Ed.). (1997). *Deconstruction in a nutshell: A conversation with Jacques Derrida*. New York: Fordham University Press.
Chadha, K., & Koliska, M. (2015). Newsrooms and transparency in the digital age. *Journalism Practice, 9*(2), 215–229.
Cunningham, B. (2006, July/August). Skin deep: When 'transparency' is a smoke screen. *Columbia Journalism Review*, 9–10.
Domingo, D. (2008). Interactivity in the daily routines of online newsrooms: Dealing with an uncomfortable myth. *Journal of Computer-Mediated Communication, 13*(3), 680–704.
Domingo, D., Quandt, T., Heinonen, A., Paulussen, S., Singer, J. B., & Vujnovic, M. (2008). Participatory journalism practices in the media and beyond: An international comparative study of initiatives in online newspapers. *Journalism Practice, 2*(3), 326–342.
Durkheim, E., & Lukes, S. (2014). *The rules of sociological method: And selected texts on sociology and its method*. New York: Free Press.
Emery, M., & Emery, E. (1996). *The press and America: An interpretive history of the mass media*. Boston: Allyn & Bacon.
Foucault, M. (1980). *Power/knowledge: Selected interviews and other writings, 1972–1977*. New York: Pantheon.
Giddens, A. (1991). *Modernity and self-identity. Self and society in the late modern age*. Stanford: Stanford University Press.
Gregg, M. (2011). *Work's intimacy*. Cambridge: Polity Press.
Hedman, U., & Djerf-Pierre, M. (2013). The social journalist. *Digital Journalism, 1*(3), 368–385.
Heinonen, A. (2011). The journalist's relationship with users: New dimensions to conventional roles. In J. B. Singer, D. Domingo, A. Heinonen, A. Hermida, S. Paulussen, T. Quandt, Z. Reich, & M. Vujnovic (Eds.), *Participatory journalism: Guarding open gates at online newspapers* (pp. 34–55). West Sussex: Wiley.

Hermida, A. (2012). Tweets and truth: Journalism as a discipline of collaborative verification. *Journalism Practice, 6*(5–6). Retrieved from http://www.tandfonline.com/doi/abs/10.1080/17512786.2012.667269.

Hiltzik, M. (2015, March 24). How should journalists treat candidates who deny climate change. *LA Times*. Retrieved from http://www.latimes.com/business/hiltzik/la-fi-mh-how-should-reporters-treat-candidates-who-deny-climate-change-20150324-column.html.

Holton, A. E., & Molyneux, L. (2015). Identity lost? The personal impact of brand journalism. *Journalism*. doi:10.1177/1464884915608816.

Karlsson, M. (2008, May). *Visibility of journalistic processes and the undermining of objectivity*. Paper presented at 21st International Communication Association conference, Montreal. Retrieved from http://research.allacademic.com/meta/p_mla_apa_research_citation/2/3/1/7/9/p231799_index.html.

Koenig, S. (lead producer). (2014). *Serial* [podcast]. Retrieved from https://serialpodcast.org/.

Küng, L. (2015). *Innovators in digital news*. London: I.B Tauris.

Larson, S. (2014, October 9). Serial: The podcast we've been waiting for. *The New Yorker*. Retrieved from http://www.newyorker.com/culture/sarah-larson/serial-podcast-weve-waiting.

Lasorsa, D. L., Lewis, S. C., & Holton, A. (2012). Normalizing Twitter: Journalism practice in an emerging communication space. *Journalism Studies, 13*(1), 19–36.

Last Week Tonight with John Oliver. (2014, May 11). *YouTube*. Retrieved from https://www.youtube.com/watch?v=cjuGCJJUGsg.

Lewis, S. (2012). The tension between professional control and open participation. *Information, Communication & Society, 15*(6), 836–866.

Lippmann, W. (1920). *Liberty and the news*. New Brunswick, NJ: Transaction Publishers.

Lowe, A. (2012, September 28). Trial by social media worry in Jill Meagher case. *The Sydney Morning Herald*. Retrieved from http://www.smh.com.au/technology/technology-news/trial-by-social-media-worry-in-meagher-case-20120928-26pe4.html.

Mandiberg, M. (2012). Introduction. In M. Mandiberg (Ed.), *The social media reader*. New York: New York University Press.

Marwick, A. (2013). *Status update: Celebrity, publicity, and branding in the social media age*. New Haven: Yale University Press.

Marwick, A. (2015). Instafame: Luxury selfies in the attention economy. *Public Culture, 27*, 137–160.

Marwick, A. E., & boyd, d. (2011). I tweet honestly, I tweet passionately: Twitter users, context collapse, and the imagined audience. *New Media & Society, 13*(1), 114–133.

Mindich, D. (1998). *Just the facts: How objectivity came to define American Journalism*. New York: New York University Press.
Paulussen, S. (2016). Innovation in the newsroom. In T. Witschge, C. Anderson, & D. Domingo (Eds.), *The SAGE handbook of digital journalism* (pp. 192–206). London: Sage.
Reed, A. (2005). 'My Blog is Me': Texts and persons in UK online journal culture (and anthropology). *Ethnos, 70*(2), 220–242.
Russell, A. (2016). Networked journalism. In T. Witschge, C. Anderson, & D. Domingo (Eds.), *The SAGE handbook of digital journalism* (pp. 149–163). London: Sage.
Schudson, M. (1978). *Discovering the news: A social history of American newspapers*. New York: Basic Books.
Schudson, M. (2011). *The sociology of news*. New York: W.W Norton.
Shapiro, I., Brin, C., Bédard-Brûlé, I., & Mychajlowycz, K. (2013). Verification as a strategic ritual. *Journalism Practice, 7*(6). Retrieved from: http://www.tandfonline.com.ezproxy.lib.swin.edu.au/doi/full/10.1080/17512786.2013.765638.
Shoemaker, P. J., Vos, T., & Reece, S. (2009). Journalists as gatekeepers. In K. Wahl-Jorgensen & T. Hanitzch (Eds.), *The handbook of journalism studies* (pp. 73–88). New York: Routledge.
Simons, M. (2007). *The content makers: Understanding the media in Australia*. Melbourne: Penguin.
Singer, J. (2005). The political J-blogger: 'Normalising' a new media form to fit old norms and practices. *Journalism, 6*(2), 173–198.
Singer, J. (2007). Contested autonomy—Professional and popular claims on journalistic norms. *Journalism Studies, 8*, 79–95.
Sterne, P. (2016, January 28). Huffpost to publish anti-Trump kicker with all Trump coverage. *Politico*. Retrieved from http://www.politico.com/blogs/on-media/2016/01/huffpost-to-publish-anti-trump-kicker-with-all-trump-coverage-218345.
Tandoc, E. C., & Vos, T. (2016). The journalist is marketing the news: Social media in the gatekeeping process. *Journalism Practice, 10*(8), 950–966.
Tuchman, G. (1972). Objectivity as strategic ritual: An examination of newsmen's notions of objectivit`y. *American Journal of Sociology, 77*, 660–679.
Tuchman, G. (1978). *Making news: A study in the construction of reality*. New York: The Free Press.
Turner, D. (2012, July 6). Inside the BBC's verification hub. *Nieman Reports*. Retrieved from http://niemanreports.org/articles/inside-the-bbcs-verification-hub/.
Vocational Guidance Bureau. (1964). *Journalism*. Orange, NSW: Department of Labour and Industry NSW.

Vos, T., & Craft, S. (2016). The discursive construction of journalistic transparency. *Journalism Studies*. Retrieved from http://www.tandfonline.com/doi/abs/10.1080/1461670X.2015.1135754.

Wahl-Jorgensen, K. (2013). The strategic ritual of emotionality: A case study of Pulitzer Prize-winning articles. *Journalism, 14*(1), 129–145.

Walker, R. B. (1976). *The newspaper press in NSW, 1803–1920*. Sydney: Sydney University Press.

Zelizer, B. (2004). *Taking journalism seriously: News and the academy*. Thousand Oaks, CA: Sage.

Zielinski, C. (2013, September 30). Thousands march to remember Jill Meagher. *The Age*. Retrieved from http://www.theage.com.au/victoria/thousands-march-to-remember-jill-meagher-20130929-2umj1.html.

CHAPTER 3

Journalism and Social Media Audiences

Tahrir Square quietly celebrated an anniversary on January 2016—it had been five years since the popular uprisings that toppled Egypt's Mubarak government and brought a global audience to major political rebellions occurring across the Middle East. However, this anniversary was not at all reminiscent of the highly mediated public protests of 2011. Instead, a crackdown on any form of public dissent, including raids on the homes of activists and even outlawing street vendors in Tahrir Square, indicated the new Egyptian government's attitude towards this public anniversary. While major news organisations published some commemorative feature articles and *Al Jazeera* (Arab Spring Protesters 2016) reported that smaller groups of anti-government protesters had formed on the day of the anniversary, media reportage was nowhere near the global phenomenon that had created the 'Arab Spring' five years previously.

The so-called Arab Spring began in Tunisia in 2010, as a public response to the self-immolation of street vendor Mohamed Bouaziz, which brought large-scale protests about government corruption to the country. The ferocity of the protests resulted in the resignation of President Zine El Abidine Ben Ali and sparked popular uprisings in Libya, Yemen, Syria, Egypt and other countries. It was the protests in Egypt that inspired much of the global media's attention, because well-organised and media-savvy activist groups were also working to publicise and document the protests on social media. Both academic and media commentators drew attention to the seemingly collaborative relationship protesters had with international journalists to report upon daily events

D. Bossio, *Journalism and Social Media*,
DOI 10.1007/978-3-319-65472-0_3

and social issues in Egypt more broadly. Some of the more hyperbolic analysis described a 'social media revolution', where traditional media audiences gained some control of the news agenda by sharing thousands of eyewitness accounts, videos, tweets and *Facebook* posts on social media platforms, rather than through traditional media (Lister and Smith 2011; Lotan et al. 2011).

Five years has shown both the oversimplification of a 'social media revolution' and, more importantly, the inherent complexity of the relationship between news organisations, journalists and their audiences. While subsequent analysis of the Arab Spring has shown evidence of journalist and citizen collaborations for reportage (Bossio 2014), as well as innovative use of citizen-focussed reportage (Bruns et al. 2012), the reality of social media-enabled interactions between journalists and citizens was rather more limited. Similarly, the Egyptian, Tunisian and Libyan people have faced difficulties affecting social change subsequent to the fervour of revolution—and away from the glare of international media attention.

While the previous chapter focussed on journalistic practice in social media environments, this chapter explores the traditional 'recipients' of journalism—the news media audience. In particular, the apparent empowerment of audiences on social media and the dominance of their preferences in the production and consumption of news (Anderson 2011, p. 557). The traditional news audience has always been active and dynamic—news audiences have always commented, interpreted and shared news. Letters to the editor in local newspapers and community notice boards are traditional reminders of the active nature of audiences. However, the emergence of digital, online and social media-enabled environments has changed the traditionally 'one-way' communication relationship between journalists and their audiences, making it possible for audiences to 'talk back' by commenting, sharing and even making their own media content (Bruns 2007). Similarly, the traditional conception of audiences as a unified mass has been overtaken by distributed networks, niche groupings and issue-oriented audiences on social media (Heinrich 2011). This has led to a conceptual change in the representation of news audiences, from 'passive consumers of news that needed to be given "the information they needed" by professional journalists', to an empowered force for the co-creation and distribution of news (Anderson 2011, p. 564). Academic and industry research has also taken an 'audience turn' (Lee and Chyi 2014), analysing the different ways the audience has become part of the journalistic process. Some research has shown that increased audience interaction via social media has provided new reportage opportunities for journalists (Lee et al. 2014). Others have suggested that these interactions may be useful during coverage of specific events or issues, but tensions emerge in transitioning these interactions to an overall professional or organisational approach to audience engagement (Hedman and Djerf-Pierre 2013).

While much of this research has focussed on how a more engaged audience has created changes in the production and distribution of news, this chapter will focus more broadly on the ways in which public dialogue has changed. Public dialogue is defined as deliberate, participatory engagement with an event or issue by a diverse mix of public participants in order to share knowledge and experiences. Importantly, this engagement does not require uniformity of opinion, nor a shared outcome, but merely a connection through participation in the topic. This is important within online and social media spaces, where traditional social constructs, such as the nation, break down and 'new knowledge communities' emerge based on voluntary, temporary, and strategic groupings (Jenkins and Ito 2015). Members of these communities shift as their interests develop, or they belong to multiple knowledge communities, each being sustained by the common need for production and exchange of particular kinds of public dialogue. Bruns and Burgess (2011) define these connections on social media as 'ad hoc publics', where short-term networks or groups for discussion might appear around particular events, posts or content and some users might become influential through their engagement with these topics or events. Ad hoc publics are not static, and may change or become part of established online communities over time. Within these social media spaces, news becomes a distributed conversation in which a number of individuals are responding simultaneously to events as a kind of 'ambient journalism' (Hermida 2011). Social media interactions between users can thus be seen as an aggregated form of journalistic content, experienced as a constant ambient presence in social media spaces, but becoming more explicit when major news breaks. Shaw et al. (2013, p. 23) suggest this results in a 'public and collective' expression of public dialogue about particular news events, either without the need for input from professional journalists, or in connection with traditional news organisations.

The ideal of this participatory communication is the creation of online publics that allow for dynamic civic engagement with social and cultural issues (Jenkins 2006). This ideal has often been framed by the representation of unified groups working collaboratively within networks to debate and to affect change (Livingstone 2005). However, the reality of the emergence of this participatory online culture has been much more complex and heterogeneous. In particular, traditional norms of public dialogue framed by professional ideologies, and governmental and legal norms have become sites of contestation in online and social media spaces, as audiences resist or recreate the power structures that framed public engagement, sometimes in deliberately 'uncivil' ways, such as trolling or satirical hoaxes. In the context of journalism, online and social media have changed the nature of dialogue between journalists and audiences, creating new spaces for the audience to critique, re-present, dismiss, or even completely ignore the journalist.

This chapter argues that this has changed public dialogue, especially the roles of participants, and the 'rules of engagement' in participatory forms of social media communication. Crawford (2009, p. 528) suggests that online spaces create interconnections through 'access to the details of someone's everyday life, as prosaic as they often are, which contributes to the sense of "ambient intimacy" in social media'. This constant access to ambient intimacy, as well as the dominance of affective content based on personal opinion and experience, and, finally, the centrality of the user in the construction of ad hoc publics engaged with issues and events of interest creates public spaces and communities with very different cultures, politics and rules of civil engagement. McCosker (2014) argues that 'a truly pluralistic participatory experience includes not just being affected by new forms and flows of networked media content and communication, but also the power to affect with new forms of reciprocal capacity to act out and even "act up"'. For many users, emotional, satirical and even combative forms of engagement with news events are simply a way of participating in information flows as part of a broader sense of social media communication culture—participation and contribution to social and cultural life through the particular affordances of social media. However, this communication culture differs exponentially from the tightly governed, structured forms of communication created by traditional norms of professional journalism.

This chapter uses a case study of the Egyptian Arab Spring to chart these changes, proceeding firstly by illustrating how the definition of the news audience has changed, and secondly by contextualising the new audience–journalist relationship through the norms of professional practice established in the previous chapter. The changes that have occurred in this relationship since the introduction of social media forms of communication are also discussed, such as new audience-led forms of journalism. Finally, using examples from reportage of the Arab Spring sets the context for understanding some of the opportunities and challenges that social media-led interactions with traditional audiences can bring to both journalistic practice and public dialogue and engagement more broadly.

How 'Audiences' Have Changed—a Problem of Definition

Much of the international reportage about the Arab Spring protests throughout 2011 and 2012 reflected the hopeful determination so proudly displayed by protesters in Egypt's Tahrir Square. Despite days of social upheaval and violence, many professional journalists reported that the activists' demands for 'bread, freedom and social justice' would surely be met (Yassin-Kassab et al. 2016). Hosni Mubarak's resignation from his presidency almost 20 days into the protests seemed to confirm the push towards social reform in the country. Five years later, much of that hopeful determination has turned to despair. News reports documenting the rise and fall of President Mohammad Morsi, the outlawing of the Muslim Brotherhood, rigged elections and violent clashes between protesters and police have marred the optimism created by the Arab Spring. By 2014, the entire Egyptian government had resigned, paving the way for former army chief Abdel Fattah el-Sisi to become president. More recent news reports have detailed the jailing and disappearance of activists who came to prominence during the Arab Spring, as well as the banning of public protests and sidelining of opposition parties. As the now-jailed Egyptian activist Alaa Abd El-Fattah suggests, Egypt's Arab Spring had gone from a narrative of change to 'a dangerous cocktail of nationalist, nativist, collectivist and post-colonialist language appropriated by both sides of the conflict and used to spin convoluted conspiracy theories and spread paranoia' (Yassin-Kassab et al. 2016). Indeed, El-Fattah suggests the loss of 'hope' came with the loss of the 'narrative of revolution', a narrative that was once facilitated in part by thousands of highly educated and media-savvy young activists sharing media content, which was curated and distributed by professional journalists to worldwide audiences. Engagement of global audiences through social media and professional journalism helped to fuel this narrative, but as the fervour died down and eyeballs and hashtags turned elsewhere, the public dialogue between witnesses, reporters and audiences became much more difficult for everyday Egyptians to facilitate.

Perhaps this change in the narrative of the Arab Spring reflects the heterogeneity of various publics in social media environments. Indeed, one of the problems with describing the changes occurring between journalists and audiences on social media in the context of the Arab Spring was defining who the audience actually was. The heterogeneity of publics in social media environments means that the nature of public dialogue is also fragmented between various interests and groups. Defining the audience is not a new problem in media or journalism studies; in fact, it has been the subject of much theoretical discussion, especially since conception of the 'mediatisation' of cultural and social life through the pervasive influence of broadcast and online technologies (Hjarvard 2008). For example, Ang's (1991) work to understand industrial definition of the televisual audience illustrates the complexity of the audience's composition and actions in media spheres. Ang (1991, p. 13) refers to the actual world of audiences, not as distinct groups, but as a 'shorthand' for 'infinite, contradictory, dispersed and dynamic' experiences of television enacted in people's everyday lives. Indeed, the audience itself is a construction, socially and institutionally produced for industrial, economic and cultural aspirations (Ang 1991, p. 3). The difference between this audience construction and the reality of audience activity is the dynamism of everyday engagement with media; 'a heterogeneous range of informal activities, uses, interpretations, pleasures, disappointments, conflicts, struggles, compromises' (Ang 1991, p. 2). But the more institutional view of the audience dismisses the heterogeneity of the audience in favour of the representation of a unified group, which can be easily quantified for the purposes of creating content. This creates a power dynamic that is exploited by media producers and their organisational structures, which results in subjugating the audience (Ang 1991, p. 23). However, these previously stable, industrialised conceptions of audience have been disrupted somewhat by the social actions and interactions afforded by social media technologies.

Newer theorisations of the 'quantified' audience refer to web and social media analytics to illustrate how the relationship between journalists and audiences is being disrupted by conceptions of audiences as paradoxically productive and quantifiable. Anderson (2011, p. 551) argues that traditional conceptions of audiences as a 'quantifiable and largely consumptive aggregate' have been challenged by newer understandings of the generative qualities of online and social media audiences. Yet, as news organisations transition their practices to more audience-engaged newsrooms, there remains a tension between the increasingly prominent and widespread techniques of audience measurement, the characterisation of an active audience, and the journalist's own professional ideologies (Anderson 2011, p. 552). The use of online and social media has thus shifted the organisational understanding of the use of the audience—from a mass that needs to be fed news, to a creative force whose exact needs and preferences can be analysed to frame the news agenda. This has led to the increased organisational use of technologies that allows measurement and analysis of audiences, as well as management strategies that emphasise the subsequent audience metrics in the creation of the news agenda (Anderson 2011, p. 555). While the positive and negative impacts of social media analytics will be discussed further in Chap. 5, the use of these analytics has also impacted on the relationship between journalists and audiences.

While many journalists acknowledge the increasingly interconnected relationship between news producers and audiences, it has not always been easy to give up authority over the representation of news. For example, Hille and Bakker's (2014) research shows that journalists do not actually engage with audiences after they have published their news stories, with much of the user commentary creating conversation amongst users rather than being monitored by journalists themselves. While journalists may still resist some forms of audience participation in the news, they do acknowledge the importance of audience consumption preferences in setting the news agenda: 'Whereas reporters were once surprised by reader feedback, it seems that they now expect reader feedback, even if they do not like it, agree with it, or see it as enhancing their ultimate journalistic product' (Anderson 2011, p. 558). Furthermore, the relevance of the increased use of audience metrics is symptomatic of increasingly collaborative and quantified relations between journalists and audiences.

The organisational understanding of the social media audience has at times mimicked the industrial prioritisation of quantifiable engagements with the audience—seen in the strategic use of analytics to measure the preferences of audiences. Livingstone (2005, p. 18), suggests that quantification limits the actual dynamism of the audience: 'the effect of media on their audience is seen to reposition what was or might be or should be, a public (knowing, thinking, influential) as a mere crowd (watching, sharing and emoting) or mass of consumers (driven by tastes, preferences and motivations)'. This means that only certain groups or activities are seen as being for 'the public', while the 'audience' is merely an industrial tool, not considered as important to the functioning of society. Instead, Livingstone (2005, p. 18) suggests that conceptions of publics speak for the will of the people, while audiences are spoken to, by much larger organisational structures. This is not to say that individual users or social media content do not also have commercial or strategic interests. Rather, it is the form of communication on social media that has changed and the roles and rules of engagement within them. Conceptions of social media publics prioritise the individual expression of users and personal interconnections based on 'public and collective' expression of public affect about particular news event (Shaw et al. 2013, p. 23). Journalists, just like any other user, can become influential in these networks, but public dialogue about news on social media is no longer reliant on input from professional journalists, or connection with traditional news organisations.

The Arab Spring and Social Media Audiences

The Egyptian Arab Spring is an example of the way in which journalists' autonomy and social authority was replaced in some instances by the collaborative efforts of interested ad hoc publics on social media. While analysis of mainstream journalistic practice during the Arab Spring in Egypt has shown that mainstream news was still predominantly represented through traditional reportage of professional correspondents (Bossio and Bebawi 2013), many international journalists flying into Egypt found that their practices were disrupted by intentional bandwidth throttling by governmental agencies, as well as military-enforced curfews. However, some journalists connected with Egyptian activists who were aware of the benefits of raising awareness of the protests for international media audiences. This resulted in a mix of professional and 'non-professional' modes of news media production interacting in order to source, confirm and distribute information to both local and global audiences (Bossio and Bebawi 2013). Thus, journalists were curating

Twitter, *YouTube* and *Facebook* posts from activists, which supplemented their own coverage of the uprisings, especially during state crackdowns on journalists in Egypt.

There were also instances of mainstream journalists on social media encouraging local people to phone or email to keep journalists updated during communications blackouts. For example, *Al Jazeera English* (*AJE*) was targeted as a 'dissident' channel in Egypt, and during the initial days of protest, Egypt's Information Ministry revoked *AJE*'s media accreditation (Bossio 2014). Egyptian authorities shut down *AJE*'s Cairo bureau, and shut off satellite access to the channel (Egypt shuts down 2011). *AJE* was forced to find another satellite service outside Egypt and relied on social media to put together the news. Indeed, *AJE* was probably the most prominent of the international media organisations to prioritise both the use of social media and collaborative reportage with protesters. On the other hand, media-savvy Egyptian activists integrated their own rallying cries with hashtags; slogans for revolution were posted on social media platforms, alongside their own eyewitness reports and links to international reportage. In this environment, public dialogue shifted, incorporating much more collaborative and iterative notions of news production, as well as more dynamic information flows (Heinrich 2011, p. 62). Both the audience and the journalists took part in this collaborative mode of news production, with each participant in public dialogue becoming what Bruns (2006, p. 275) describes as a 'hybrid user-producer'.

The increasingly blurred boundaries between production and reception of news has led some to question the need for a 'professional' journalist (Berkman and Shumway 2003). Downing (2001, p. ix), for example, has argued for alternative journalistic practice as 'radical', 'grassroots' or 'community' media, though these definitions have been forwarded more as a structure of information dissemination and practice not purely focussed on journalism (Bossio and Bebawi 2013). 'Citizen' journalism has also become a popular term to describe the link between alternative news practice to forms of citizenship practice and empowerment (Rodriguez 2001, p. 20). These alternative types of journalism have a political, economic and institutional imperative to produce news 'outside mainstream media institutions and networks', working with amateurs 'who typically have little or no training or professional qualifications as journalists' (Atton and Hamilton, p. 1). Others (see Brodin 2011; Livingstone 1999) have highlighted the need for trained or professional journalists to work with amateurs to verify information and encourage adherence to particular institutional and ethical guidelines.

These debates concerning the demarcation of journalism against other types of news creation suggest the complex disruptions that have contributed to the definition of journalism in social media environments, where the edges between public dialogue and journalistic practice are somewhat blurred. During the protests in Egypt, for example, people were involved in what we might call journalistic practices: eyewitness reportage and analysis of event, as well as video, audio and social media updates. Some were paid as journalists for Egyptian media outlets, others considered themselves journalists though were not paid, some were collaborating with news organisations and others were defining what they were doing simply as important information dissemination in a time of crisis (Bossio 2014). Some were also reporting from outside Egypt itself, using online resources to 'cover' the protest. Some were not Egyptian citizens but were participating in the reportage of information through other online networks. However, only some of those people identified what they were doing as 'journalism' or media production. It is the complexity of these interactions that encapsulates the dynamism of social media cultures of communication and the mix of commercial, political and social motivations that influence them.

New Audience Conceptions for Social Media Interactions

The seeming collapse of boundaries between media users, producers, audiences and activists suggests the complexity of communicative relations during the Arab Spring. Whereas protesters embraced the information dissemination possibilities of new technologies—and were also personally invested in the outcome of the protests—journalists were reporting on use of new digital technologies as both insiders (users of social media) and outsiders (observing the use of social media by others). While some academic and media commentators were suggesting that social media use during the protests was an indication of a true 'revolution of the people', others were decrying a 'social media revolution' (Lotan et al. 2011 ; Gladwell 2010). As described above, the complexity lies in the understanding of the audience and resistance to the performance of the role traditionally ascribed to the audience in this space. The variability of both the production and consumption of social media by journalists, protestors and different audiences indicates the changing nature of public dialogue in social media environments. In the social media space, increasingly fragmented ad hoc audiences with various interests 'speak' at the same time and for different purposes, but are nonetheless 'defined' or interconnected through their interest in particular events or phenomena. Similarly, both commercial and social definitions of the audience sit alongside each other in social media spaces. While public dialogue may be the motivation for interactions on social media during the Arab Spring, activists and journalists were well aware of the economies of clicks and likes that would ensure this dialogue was heard and re-distributed. What has changed then, is the dominance of the 'public' in the sourcing, creation and distribution of news and the constant renegotiation of roles and rules within social media communication.

Baym and boyd (2012, p. 320) have suggested social media 'publicness' requires new structures of interaction and new skills to understand them. This is made more dynamic as users negotiate 'blurred boundaries, multi-layered audiences, individual attributes, the specifics of the systems they use, and the contexts of their use'. What is new about these interactions on social media is the global acceptance of users' control over the application of the affordances of social media for their own objectives and public interactions (Baym and boyd 2012, p. 321). Thus, the social media audience is different from traditional audiences because it takes for granted the 'multiple and diverse kinds of publics, counterpublics, and other emergent social arrangements...The sometimes quasi-public and other times entirely public nature of social media'. The public nature of interaction and the control of publics over use of tools within particular contexts 'makes visible processes that have always been at play, while warping them in ways that call for new literacies and strategies' (Baym and boyd 2012, p. 322). In the context of journalism, the audience for commercial, promotional and entertainment functions of news runs parallel to the political and social functions of news—the different kinds of engagements with these functions occur with different types of dialogues within various online publics and creating different opportunities and tensions—all at the same time. Thus, the change that social media environments bring to audience and journalist communicative relations is the visibility of the inherent complexity of the social, cultural and political engagement and framing of news.

Russell (2016) argues that a discussion of these different relations between journalists and online publics is inherently useful to the institution of journalism. She uses the description, popularised by Beckett (2011), 'networked journalism' to define practice as diffuse and networked. In public dialogue conducted in social media environments, the journalist still adheres to professional norms and behaviours, but the authority of the journalist within this dialogue is decentralized and diffuse. Instead, a networked journalist acts as just one node that collects, processes, and distributes (and re-distributes) information. Within an organisational structure, the journalist still acts as a 'professional', with professional norms and public interest principles motivating production of news for audiences that seek to engage with a news organisation's content, but their practice is assumed to occur simultaneously with other forms of news information gathering and dissemination. Similarly, it can be assumed that this professional practice is linked with, and sometimes even dependent on, collaboration with sources, as well as audience feedback in online environments. Thus, journalists and their various online audiences can no longer be conceptualised as separate, but as interlinked nodes in a network of news and information. A networked journalist working within various 'publics' thus contributes to new professional norms by acting as a generator, witness, and interpreter of professional journalism (Hermida 2011), re-interpreting and sharing news as part of a relationship with a number of interested publics. In this environment of journalistic production, Hamilton (2016) suggests a new kind of public audience or 'citizen witnessing', as a hybridisation of the individual with the social, the mainstream with the alternative. Rather than usurping the power of news outlets, this active production of news is a productive addition of diversity, correction and iterative processes to traditional news production (Hamilton 2016). Of course, these relations are based primarily on sharing.

As the traditional demarcations between journalist and audience collapse within social media environments, a culture of sharing encapsulates the complex, networked interactions that occur in the communication and dissemination of news on social media. The concept of online and social media sharing has its beginnings in computing, where sharing was popularised as file- or data-sharing (see John 2012). But social media platforms encourage many different forms of sharing, for many different interests. Traditional online sharing is about the communication and distribution of digital content, such as images or links. But now, sharing is much broader; sharing encapsulates the representation of life through sharing of your location, your opinion through a like, or feeling through a status update or emoticon. We generally understand sharing on social media platforms to be the consistent, daily sharing of links and videos of small bits of personal and professional news and comments. John (2012, p. 176) suggests that online sharing seems overwhelmingly positive because of the pairing with notions of strong social relations within a unified public. However, the invitation to share on social media has also been exploited by commercial and political interests that profit from individual and collective emotional capital. For example, in the context of journalism, we often think of the promotional sharing practices of journalists and organisations that bring 'eyeballs' to particular media content. However, sharing also speaks to the institutional values we place on journalism as a way to activate the democratic potential of various publics. A journalist shares news for two outcomes: firstly, the more traditional distribution of news as an informational resource, and, more recently, for the collaborative work that extends from these shared resources (Cammaerts and Couldry 2016, p. 329). Thus, sharing is a collaborative as well as a dialogic media practice that has become integral to journalism in social media environments.

Understanding and conceptualising sharing in a social media context is a way to encapsulate the social ideals of journalism practice without creating the power dynamic that maintains journalistic authority over the production and dissemination of news. While some sharing on social media platforms will undoubtedly maintain the promotional practices of professional journalists trying to find larger audiences for their content, the inclusion of various audiences in the production and dissemination of news will also allow sharing associated with a broader public dialogue. Of course, sharing within emerging news practice is constrained by several issues, especially the reproduction of existing models of journalistic practice and power structures within individual professional and organisational use of social media. There is no doubt that both journalists and their audiences are constrained by the social, governmental, technological, organisational and institutional structures that limit the ways in which they are able to interact and share on social media. For example, Bossio and Sacco (2016) suggest journalists have been asked by their organisations to refrain from posting breaking news on social media before cross-media promotion of the story has occurred. Thus, commercial and promotional frameworks placed upon public dialogue may hinder the potential for social media collaboration and sharing. Indeed, Cammaerts and Couldry (2016, p. 337) also lament that some of these new practices of sharing are instrumental because they reinforce individualistic capitalist value systems of individual sharing, rather than public dialogue. Journalists attempting to emulate the success of social media 'influencers', for example, might find it difficult to maintain both the institutional boundaries of professional journalism and the promotional imperative of social media branding (Hanusch and Bruns 2017). Thus, understanding of sharing must acknowledge the unfair distribution of possibilities to participate; uneven distribution and access to technologies, mediation of expression through the corporate structures of technology companies, and government-imposed restrictions that seek to exclude all but the already privileged from public dialogue.

Similarly, conceptions of public dialogue on social media must temper excessive emphasis on participatory and political potential of the platforms. Indeed, subsequent analysis of the Arab Spring protests found that social media use during the Arab Spring tended to be overstated (Bruns et al. 2013). Further analysis of hashtags used during the Arab Spring showed that they were only a communicative tool for the organisation of protests in the initial days of the Arab Spring and then were more likely to be used by 'elite' Arab and English-speaking users as an awareness-raising and news engagement tool (Bruns et al. 2013). On the other hand, Egyptian activists and bloggers consistently conveyed information to their readers using social media, re-tweeting coverage from the mainstream press, and occasionally criticizing the coverage, but in the main using it as a source of credible information. The media that was meant to inform protesters and activists was simultaneously conveying news and awareness in the international community through the distribution of 'alternative' or 'citizen' online and social media reportage. Protesters were often aware of this process, directing tweets to ensure that major news organisations were covering parts of the crisis where activists had an interest in amplifying coverage.

Both media producers and audiences are constrained by the commercial, political and social limits placed on the use of social media. Within social media environments, the use of different forms of literacies, languages and cultural norms to describe news events and issues creates both possibilities and tensions in the communicative relations between journalists and audiences. This does not necessarily always have negative outcomes—social media is a space that makes visible the complexity and diversity of voices in the public sphere and provides for interaction and collaboration on certain issues, though not on others. In social media environments, audiences share, comment on, critique, interpret, and add content and witness statements, or even ignore news content altogether. Use of social media is innovative at times and, at others, limited by different social, organisational and governmental contexts. Thus, as Livingstone (2005, p. 31) suggests, a news audience is 'generally neither so passive and accepting as traditionally supposed by those who denigrate them, nor generally so organised and effective as to meet the high standards of those defining public participation'. Active participation of audiences in media production and dissemination does not mean that audiences have 'ultimate power' in communicative relations, or even on social media. Indeed, Fiske and Hancock (2016) suggest the audience's power is not necessarily to change media production or institutional structures, but simply to negotiate the effects of those structures within the context of their interest and need. Perhaps the biggest difference in social media environments is that audiences interact within a number of different publics or groups, with new forms of dialogue and participation required for each. Using social media as the framework for communication, audiences are also producers, witnesses, participators and publics at the same time and, thus, the traditional contexts for—and controls over—public dialogue collapse in these spaces.

While evidence of sustained collaboration between journalists and audiences within social media environments is currently somewhat rare, the development of these smaller, 'rolling' moments of sharing is still constitutive of changes in the institutional conception of journalism. Indeed, the interactions between various publics and journalists, especially concerning crisis events, shows that journalists have been able to curate a myriad of stories for particular audiences through the interaction with particular networks (Bossio and Bebawi 2013). While Bennett and Segerberg (2013, p. 214) suggest we still do not know what 'a successful transition [to social media] looks like', this does not mean that this transition is not occurring—the dynamic and heterogeneous use of social media both by journalists and audiences will ensure that we cannot predict what it will look like, nor the 'correctness' of how it will come about. As these changes occur, we are reminded by Livingstone (2005, p. 32) that changes in the way audiences and journalists interact may not be the 'ideal', but social media interactions will occur in rather the same constrained and limited ways as other 'new' media have allowed: 'That, after all, is the point: it is precisely such context-dependent yet under-determined, plural and hybrid identities, understandings, practices and relationships that must and do shape people's engagement with others, in private and in public.'

Conclusion

The Arab Spring protests were the result of repressive social and governmental policies that inflicted hardship, especially on young people, in the countries affected. Perhaps global audiences would not have been so aware of this plight without the collaborative efforts of local activists, journalists and everyday Egyptians documenting their struggle online and on social media. Local organisation of protests and action was undoubtedly reliant on local networks of activists, but the global reach of these protests, fuelled by mainstream news reportage, was also assisted by social media like *Facebook* and *Twitter*, especially when reportage was increasingly difficult due to communications blackouts. The Arab Spring protests are one of the first examples of clear collaboration between journalists and various publics not only to create media content, but to ensure its wide dissemination through processes of sharing such as 'hashtagging', personal appeals for information and use of witness statements and amateur media content as part of reportage.

The Arab Spring protests illustrates that the conception of the audience as a traditionally stable and unified epistemological construct is no longer adequate to describe either the relationship between journalists and audiences, nor the specific roles within it. This chapter has instead argued that social media cultures of communication have enabled new formations of public dialogue and new roles for both journalists and their audiences. The Arab Spring is an example of the complexity of these relations; journalists, media producers and various audiences all negotiated communication around particular vested interests. These interests included the social importance of exchanging particular kinds of news and information, the organisational need to inform particular audience demographics in an ethical and professional way, and even the need to develop online relationships with publics according to cultural norms of particular social media platforms. The complex interactions between journalists and publics illustrates the heterogeneous nature of social media interactions and the need to conceptualise the new forms of dialogue that occur there, especially in the news and information context.

In the next two chapters, the focus shifts from the individual practitioners and creators of journalistic content to the organisational frameworks that produce mainstream news. This part of the book takes an organisational perspective on the introduction of social media to the newsroom. This approach considers the newsroom relationships, policies and procedures that impact both the ways in which individual practitioners do their job, and the overall production and dissemination of news. Chapter 4, 'Social Media and the Newsroom: New Relationships, New Policies, New Practices', argues that while there is much variation in the ways that newsrooms have attempted to integrate social media use into the newsroom, and how journalists themselves manage those policies and procedures, it is in fact the relationship between journalistic, editorial and management staff that determines whether integration of social media in the newsroom is perceived as successful.

References

Anderson, C. W. (2011). Between creative and quantified audiences: Web metrics and changing patterns of newswork in local US newsrooms. *Journalism, 12*(5), 550–566.

Ang, I. (1991). *Desperately seeking the audience*. London: Routledge.

Arab Spring Protesters Defy Crackdown. (2016, January 26). *Al Jazeera*. Retrieved from http://www.aljazeera.com/news/2016/01/arab-spring-anniversary-protesters-defy-crackdown-160125061915269.html.

Atton, C., & Hamilton, J. (2008). *Alternative journalism*. London: Sage.

Baym, N., & boyd, d. (2012). Socially mediated publicness: An introduction. *Journal of Broadcasting & Electronic Media, 56*(3), 320–329.

Beckett, C. (2011). *SuperMedia: Saving journalism so it can save the world*. Chichester: Wiley.

Bennett, W. L., & Segerberg, A. (2013). *The logic of connective action: Digital media and the personalization of contentious politics*. Cambridge: Cambridge University Press.

Berkman, R., & Shumway, C. (2003). *Digital dilemmas: Ethical issues for online media professionals*. Iowa City: Iowa State Press.

Bossio, D. (2014). Journalism during the Arab Spring: Interactions and challenges. In S. Bebawi & D. Bossio (Eds.), *Social media and the politics of reportage: The Arab Spring*. London: Palgrave Macmillan.

Bossio, D., & Bebawi, S (2013). War of Worlds? Alternative and mainstream journalistic practices in coverage of the 'Arab Spring' protests. In J. E. Hayes, K. Battles, & W. Hilton-Morrow (Eds.), *War of the words to social media: Mediated communication in times of crisis* (pp. 189–211). New York: Peter Lang.

Bossio, D., & Sacco, V. (2016). Don't tweet this! How journalists and media organisations negotiate tensions emerging from the implementation of social media policy in newsrooms. *Digital Journalism, 5*(2), 177–193.

Brodin, S. (2011, October 21). In the aftermath of the Arab Spring revolutions, journalists ask, who is a journalist? *European Journalism Centre Magazine.* Retrieved from http://www.ejc.net/magazine.

Bruns, A. (2006). Towards produsage: Futures for user-led content production. In F. Sudweeks, H. Hrachovec, & C. Ess. (Eds.), *Proceedings of Cultural Attitudes towards Communication and Technology* (pp. 275–284). Tartu, Estonia.

Bruns, A. (2007). *Produsage: Towards a Broader Framework for User-Led Content Creation.* Paper presented at the Creativity & Cognition conference, Washington, DC. Retrieved from https://www.eprints.qut.edu.au/6623/1/6623.pdf.

Bruns, A., & Burgess, J. (2011). The use of Twitter hashtags in the formation of ad hoc publics. In *Proceedings of the 6th European Consortium for Political Research (ECPR) General Conference 2011.* University of Iceland, Reykjavik. Retrieved from https://www.eprints.qut.edu.au/46515/1/The_Use_of_Twitter_Hashtags_in_the_Formation_of_Ad_Hoc_Publics_%28final%29.pdf.

Bruns, A., Highfield, T., & Lind, R. A. (2012). Blogs, Twitter, and breaking news: The produsage of citizen journalism. *Produsing Theory in a Digital World: The Intersection of Audiences and Production in Contemporary Theory, 80*(2012), 15–32.

Bruns, A., Highfield, T., & Burgess, J. (2013). The Arab Spring and social media audiences: English and Arabic Twitter users and their networks. *American Behavioral Scientist, 57*(7), 871–898.

Cammaerts, B., & Couldry, N. (2016). Digital journalism as practice. In T. Witschge, C. Anderson, & D. Domingo (Eds.), *The SAGE Handbook of Digital Journalism* (pp. 326–340). London: Sage.

Crawford, K. (2009). Following you: Disciplines of listening in social media. *Continuum, 23*(4), 525–535.

Downing, J. (2001). *Radical Media: Rebellious Communication and Social movements.* London: Sage Publications.

Egypt shuts down Al Jazeera bureau. (2011, January 30). *Al Jazeera.* Retrieved from http://www.aljazeera.com/news/middleeast/2011/01/201113085252994161.html.

Fiske, J., & Hancock, B. H. (2016). *Power plays power works* (2nd ed.). New York: Routledge.

Gladwell, M. (2010, October 4). Small Change: Why the revolution will not be tweeted. *The New Yorker.* Retrieved from http://www.newyorker.com/magazine/2010/10/04/small-change-malcolm-gladwell.

Hamilton, J. (2016). Hybrid news practices. In T. Witschge, C. Anderson, & D. Domingo (Eds.), *The SAGE Handbook of digital Journalism* (Vol. 55, pp. 164–178). London: Sage.

Hanusch, F., & Bruns, A. (2017). Journalistic Branding on Twitter. *Digital Journalism, 5*(1). Retrieved from http://www.tandfonline.com/doi/full/10.1080/21670811.2016.1152161.

Hedman, U., & Djerf-Pierre, M. (2013). The social journalist. *Digital. Journalism, 1*(3), 368–385.

Heinrich, A. (2011). *Network Journalism: Journalistic Practice in Interactive Spheres.* Hoboken, NY: Routledge.

Hermida, A. (2011). Fluid spaces, fluid journalism: Lessons in participatory journalism. In Jane B. Singer, D. Domingo, A. Heinonen, A. Hermida, S. Paulussen, T. Quandt, et al. (Eds.), *Participatory journalism: Guarding open gates at online newspapers* (pp. 177–191). Malden, MA: Wiley-Blackwell.

Hille, S., & Bakker, P. (2014). Engaging the social news user: Comments on news sites and Facebook. *Journalism Practice, 8*(5), 563–572.

Hjarvard, S. (2008). The Mediatisation of society: A Theory of the Media as Agents of Social and Cultural Change. *Nordicom Review, 29*(2), 105–134.

Jenkins, H. (2006). *Convergence culture: Where old and new media collide.* New York: NYU press.

Jenkins, H., & Ito, M. (2015). *Participatory culture in a networked era: A conversation on youth, learning, commerce, and politics.* Chichester: Wiley.

John, N. A. (2012). Sharing and Web 2.0: The emergence of a keyword. *New Media & Society, 15*(2), 167–182.

Lee, A. M., & Chyi, H. I. (2014). When Newsworthy is Not Noteworthy: Examining the value of news from the audience's perspective. *Journalism Studies, 15*(6), 807–820.

Lee, A. M., Lewis, S. C., & Powers, M. (2014). Audience clicks and news placement: A study of time-lagged influence in online journalism. *Communication Research, 41*(4), 505–530.

Lister, T., & Smith, E. (2011, January 27). Social media @the frontline in Egypt. *CNN.* Retrieved from http://edition.cnn.com/2011/WORLD/africa/01/27/egypt.protests.social.media/.

Livingstone, S. (1999). New media, new audiences? *New Media and Society, 1*(1), 59–66.

Livingstone, S. (2005). Audiences and publics: When cultural engagement matters for the public sphere. *Changing Media, Changing Europe Series.* Bristol: Intellect.

Lotan, G., Graeff, E., Ananny, M., Gaffney, D., & Pearce, I. (2011). The Arab Spring: The revolutions were tweeted: Information flows during the 2011

Tunisian and Egyptian revolutions. *International journal of communication, 5*. Retrieved from http://www.ijoc.org/index.php/ijoc/article/view/1246
McCosker, A. (2014). Trolling as provocation: YouTube's agonistic publics. *Convergence: The International Journal of Research into New Media Technologies, 20*(2), 201–217.
Rodriguez, C. (2001). *Fissures in the mediascape: An international study of citizens' media*. Cresskill, NJ: Hampton Press.
Russell, A. (2016). Networked journalism. In T. Witschge, C. Anderson, & D. Domingo (Eds.), *The SAGE Handbook of digital Journalism* (pp. 149–163). London: Sage.
Shaw, F., Burgess, J., Crawford, K., & Bruns, A. (2013). Sharing news, making sense, saying thanks. *Australian Journal of Communication, 40*(1), 23–39.
Yassin-Kassab, R., Abd El Fattah, A., Soueif, A., Barghouti, M., Lalami, L., Shehadeh, R., et al. (2016, January 23). I was terribly wrong—writers look back on the Arab Spring Five years on. *The Guardian*. Retrieved from: https://www.theguardian.com/books/2016/jan/23/arab-spring-five-years-on-writers-look-back.

CHAPTER 4

Social Media and the Newsroom: New Relationships, New Policies, New Practices

During October 2016, the *Australian Broadcasting Corporation*'s (*ABC*) head of editorial policy, Alan Sunderland, found himself having to defend the organisation's approach to investigative journalism. The *ABC* television programme *Four Corners* had just broadcast an investigative feature on the lives of asylum seekers being detained by the Australian government on Nauru, showing substandard living conditions, including poor sanitation, educational facilities and medical resources (Whitmont and Harley 2016). The report used interviews with adults and children who had been in detention on the island, as well as reports from organisations such as *Save the Children* and *Amnesty International*, which were damning of the facilities and the detention process overall. Immediately following the programme, the Nauruan government issued a press release labelling the *ABC* 'an embarrassment to journalism', and accused the broadcaster's report of containing racist political activism (Statement 2016). Further to this criticism, the Australian Immigration Minister Peter Dutton, claimed that journalists working at the *ABC* were 'advocates dressed up as journalists' (Knott 2016). *ABC* executives were eventually called to a Senate Estimates hearing by Liberal Senator for Victoria, Jane Hume, to answer charges of bias. Senator Hume asked Sunderland why no *ABC* journalist had travelled to Nauru for the story, and why footage was filmed by a third party at the programme's request (ABC Defends 2016). The senator suggested that the *ABC* was, at times, too reliant on 'activist organisations' for its content, and called

D. Bossio, *Journalism and Social Media*,
DOI 10.1007/978-3-319-65472-0_4

for the *ABC's* managing director, Michelle Guthrie, to launch an inquiry into the programme (ABC Defends 2016).

Sunderland stood by the programme, saying that the broadcaster would not 'launch inquiries into excellent pieces of journalism' (Knott 2016). Mr. Sunderland's responses to the senator's questions revealed some of the organisational processes for investigative journalism at the *ABC*. Sunderland said all interviews were conducted remotely by freelance journalists because the Nauruan government charged prohibitive fees for media visas and regularly refused journalists access to the offshore processing centres. He also claimed that all stories were subjected to rigorous fact-checking processes, and that the newsroom adhered to strict editorial standards. In the wake of the scandal, some *Four Corners* journalists also took to social media to illustrate the 'behind the scenes' organisational and journalistic approach to the investigation. For example, *Four Corners*' executive producer, Sally Neighbour, revealed on *Twitter* that the programme had approached Immigration Minister Peter Dutton for an interview about the detention centres on Nauru, but he had only wanted to be interviewed live—which the programme was unable to do due to their programming limitations (Koziol 2016).

In Chap. 2, use of social media was shown to enable transparency in journalism, often revealing the processes and decision-making 'behind the curtain' of the professional news product. In this example of governmental criticism of journalistic processes, an interesting insight into the organisations that create journalism was also revealed. Indeed, Sally Neighbour's tweet shows how the more informal characteristics of some social media platforms enable this 'behind the scenes' understanding of the newsroom and, thus, reveals how organisational structures, policies and approaches to practice might influence journalistic products. The Senates Estimates hearing illustrated, for example, how the public broadcaster used freelance and casual journalists, how it approached processes of verification and its editorial approach to investigative journalism, all of which had an effect on what was produced on *Four Corners*. Therefore, it is important to take into consideration the organisational structures, policies and approaches that might shape or influence the way social media is used (and limited) both by individual journalists and news organisations themselves.

Previous research has focussed on the transition of individual journalistic practice to include social media engagement, but less attention has been given to the ways organisational strategies might contribute to the use of these practices. The previous chapter explored journalists' relationships with audiences in social media environments, discussing the ways in which public dialogue is influenced by the use of social media tools. This chapter now moves into an exploration of how these interactions and their outcomes are influenced by the structures and practices of the news organisations within which journalists work. This chapter focusses on the new professional relationships, policies and procedures that have been introduced to structure both the individual and organisational use of social media in the newsroom.

While new digital and online capabilities have fundamentally disrupted both the business model and production processes of mainstream news organisations, I argue that the impact of social media can be seen more in the new relations between journalists and other stakeholders in the newsroom. There is much variation in the ways organisations have attempted to integrate social media use into the newsroom. However, the success of its introduction is largely determined by relations between journalistic, editorial and management staff. Thus, the impact of social media on the newsroom is not primarily economic, but manifests instead in journalists' prioritisation of either strategic or editorial uses of social media in their practice. At its best, the introduction of social media has created productive new relations in the newsroom and new ways to source and promote news and information. At its worst, social media acts as a 'perverse incentive', prioritising and quantifying clicks and shares as a journalistic marker of quality, rather than its value within public dialogue. These effects influence the news product itself and, indirectly, the potential of social media use in news organisations.

Much of the context for understanding the organisational impact on news has been economic—understanding the changing business models that support the production of journalism. While this is important, this chapter moves away from this focus to a broader examination of how the production of news is managed, strategised and staffed, and how this has changed to account for the growing impact of social media in online news distribution and consumption. This chapter favours the impact of interrelations between the different stakeholders in the newsroom and their management and negotiation of strategies for using social media in the production of news. Comparative examples from the introduction of online and social media production at another Australian news organisation, *The Age* newspaper in Melbourne, will illustrate different relations between management and editorial staff in order to understand whether those procedures were perceived as successful.

The Business of Journalism

The use of social media has changed some news production, distribution and consumption processes in a relatively short period of time. In 2014, Nielsen and Schrøder reported that a survey of eight European countries showed that 'social media at this point still play a relatively limited role as sources of news—less widely used and less important than printed newspapers'. Just two years later, a larger report showed a fundamental shift, both in the production and consumption of news; almost half of the people surveyed said they used social media as a source of news, and one in ten said it was their main source of news (Newman 2016). The report suggests that across the 26 countries surveyed, the one commonality for legacy news organisations was 'job losses, cost-cutting, and missed targets as falling print revenues combine with the brutal economics of digital in a perfect storm' (Newman 2016).

Much of the recent research focus on journalism and news organisations has been on the (often failing) 'economics' of producing news. Two issues have dominated this discussion—how many journalists have left the profession due to financial cutbacks within the organisation (Zion et al. 2016) and which business models might bring profits back to news organisations in the digital age. The latter has been especially pertinent to discussion of how legacy news organisations would 'survive' the rise of digital and online publishing and communication. Indeed, the extent of change in the economic fortunes of established news organisations has been both swift and all-encompassing. The news media business, as summarised by Simons (2007, p. 5), was once a simple and profitable business model: 'Journalists and editors produced content that people wanted to read and view, and distributed it thanks to privileged access to printing presses and broadcasting licenses. The publishers or broadcasters were then able to sell the audience to advertisers. Money was made, and some of it was reinvested in journalism. Simple, and mostly good.' The introduction of online communication technologies meant that privileged access to the means to produce and disseminate media dissipated, along with the advertising 'rivers of gold' that supported it. The increasing popularity of shareable media, such as blogs and microblogging platforms, smartphone text messaging, and image and sound recording capabilities, meant that, suddenly, everyone had the means to capture the daily minutiae of life and render them 'news'.

While the social changes that stemmed from the onset of online and social media communication tools have been mostly celebrated, their deleterious effects on the traditional journalism business model have been nothing short of momentous. In the USA alone, hundreds of daily newspapers have folded, thousands of journalists have been made redundant, and concerns about the lack of quality investigative journalism have been increasing (Tiffen 2010). Print circulation in the USA has been falling 5–8% per year, though in some cases circulation revenue has increased due to price increases (Edmonds 2016). *PricewaterhouseCoopers*' (Global Entertainment 2016) annual industry outlook report for 2016 indicated that newspaper revenue in Western Europe and North America will continue to fall, and the slowing economic outlook for China will result in an annual circulation decline of 0.7% to 2020 (Global Entertainment 2016). Only Latin America is projected to increase revenues in traditional media, helped largely by the region's economic growth overall, as well as successful strategies for paid digital content. Despite pockets of growth, and the increase of small, online-only and niche journalism that has filled some of the gaps left by declining print media, concern about loss of plurality (Carson 2015) and resulting superficiality of news continues to grow.

This change in the fortunes of legacy news media can be seen as a failure of its traditional business model (Picard 2010). Legacy news organisations have significant fixed costs based on their long-established journalistic services, but the declining print revenue and advertising dollar that traditionally supported journalism has meant that news has become a low-margin business (Küng 2015). News organisations have needed to find other ways to support journalism and resolve the question of how to do this in an age when 'anyone can be a journalist'. To this end, significant industry investment has been made in the development of 'paywall' systems, with varied success. Whereas news organisations had been providing free news content online, the subsequent cannibalisation of circulation revenue has prompted more than half of US newspaper organisations, and almost all Australian newspapers, to implement paywalls. Paywalls can either prevent free access to all online news content, or allow for limited access, without charge. Niche or 'premium' content is accessed via payment or subscription only. 'Soft' paywalls have been designed to allow some access to websites as a way to keep eyeballs on a news website and present stronger audience metrics to advertisers. Both forms of paywalls are designed to support the production of journalism in lieu of declining advertising revenues. While paywall implementation is increasing globally, researchers like Carson (2015) have suggested that paywalls do not earn enough to abandon print circulation altogether—but the increasing digital subscriptions also eat into potential print subscription revenue, particularly in countries with relatively small populations. Other models of subsidising the expensive work of quality journalism are clearly needed.

Some researchers (see Levy and Picard 2011) have suggested that non-profit, trust or charitable business models might be a good way to resource the production of news, with smaller news organisations, like *ProPublica*, indicating the success of this model. Some of the benefits of alternative forms of ownership include audiences being more willing to pay for specialised news reportage, and the economic benefits and tax breaks associated with certain non-profit business models (Levy and Picard 2011). While there have been some examples of successful trusts and charitable business models in countries with large populations, non-profit news has been less successful in places with smaller readerships like Australia. For example, *The Global Mail*, an Australian not-for-profit news site supported with philanthropic funding from Internet entrepreneur, Graeme Wood, only lasted two years despite winning a number of awards for journalism—and Wood initially committing to funding for five years (Meade 2014). A number of other business models have also been used to support journalism, including email syndication, corporate sponsorship, branded content and community foundation support (Picard 2014). However, Picard (2014, p. 502) suggests that these models have very similar financial imperatives to privately owned news organisations and would still need to find a way to support increasing costs if the business expanded. Any costs incurred by the production of journalism must be supplemented with an income—issues that both legacy and new organisations face (Levy and Picard 2011). These issues, coupled with the lack of a unified strategy for business planning and innovation (Küng 2015) often create issues for the successful functioning of legacy news organisations, especially when new communication practices and technologies are introduced to the newsroom.

Legacy news organisations have gone through significant upheaval during the introduction and integration of digital and web technologies in the newsroom. Indeed, the introduction of social media to newsrooms could be seen as relatively smooth compared with the period of upheaval that enveloped mainstream news organisations when faced with the technological and social change represented by online publishing. Many legacy news organisations were slow to embrace the online publishing revolution, either reluctantly introducing online capabilities, or experimenting unsuccessfully with changing journalistic processes and practices in the newsroom. *The Age* newspaper in Melbourne, Australia, introduced online capability to the newsroom around 1995 with a single computer terminal that journalists could use to gain access to the Internet (R. Myer, personal communication, 31 March 2017). *The Age's* parent company, *Fairfax*, then introduced several online 'experiments', the first being a standalone online publication called *f2*. The publication was introduced amid some controversy in the newsroom; the online journalists were considered to be separate from the newspaper and sat in a different part of the newsroom, 'shovelling' or re-writing newspaper content for online publication, sometimes without citing the original journalist (L. Schwartz, personal communication, 23 March 2017). Some journalists were said to be frustrated with these attempts at aggregation and the possibility of increased demands on their labour for online content (L. Schwartz, personal communication, 23 March 2017). More importantly, journalists saw the newly branded entity through the institutional lens of professional journalism, as a 'low rent' experiment that could not aspire to the reputation and professionalism created by the newspaper journalists (R. Myer, personal communication, 31 March 2017). At the time, online publication was considered part of the amateur practices of bloggers and this attitude was extended to the mostly young journalists and producers employed at *f2*.

The new brand was troubled from the beginning, largely due to the competing editorial and business priorities of the *f2* venture (Frew 2003). Initially wanting to capitalise on the early dotcom boom in online advertising, this business focus was soon hampered by more editorial-focussed issues of reputation and content. Despite employing a search specialist to improve the odds of searches hitting an *f2* site, the new brand made $100 million in losses in five years (Lowe 2002; Long 2002). In 2004, *Fairfax* finally ditched the brand. *Fairfax*'s CEO suggested that there was low awareness of the *f2* brand among advertisers and audiences did not make a connection from the website to their stable of reputable newspapers including *The Age*, *The Sydney Morning Herald* and *The Australian Financial Review* (f2 changes name 2004).

While *Fairfax* was initially unsuccessful in creating online news, it had much more success with other online ventures. For example, *Fairfax* acquired the online accommodation company *Stayz* for A$12.7 million in 2005, later selling it in 2013 for $220 million, far exceeding its estimated value of $140 million (Johnston 2013). Other ventures, such as an online property guide and car classified site, have also been valuable assets to the news company. However, it took several years and a dotcom crash for *Fairfax* to integrate digital and online content creation with the rest of the newsroom. The newsroom now has a mostly integrated digital newsroom, with journalists working across all platforms. Large investments have been made in video journalism, and in 2016 the company launched its first podcast with three investigative journalists from *The Age* (Bennett 2016).

The mixed success of *Fairfax*'s online ventures is fairly typical of the fraught market in which news media organisations now find themselves. Indeed, it is difficult to compare the financial successes of digital and online-only news organisations with legacy media, given differences such as size, editorial strategy and the demographic differences in readership. Küng's (2015) research into the economic and structural management of new digital-only news organisations showed that quality leadership often forms the core of a well-functioning digital newsroom. She (2015) argues that the success of new digital, online and social media-enabled newsrooms is dependent on a blending of 'journalistic, technological, and commercial competencies', as well as a 'pro-digital culture' in the newsroom. Thus, within newer online-only media organisations, commitment to professional ideologies around the public service benefits of journalism, mixed with an open-mindedness about new uses for digital, online and social media, have led to successful innovations in legacy and mainstream newsrooms.

If we compare this with a legacy news organisation such as *The Age*, the process of change has been much slower; online and social media production and practices have tended to be incremental, augmenting existing newsroom practices and framed by more traditional editorial and economic decision making. The successful transition of large news media organisations like *The Age* to social media environments has sometimes been hampered by their 'legacy' structures, processes and culture. Where larger organisations might expect workers to adhere to their long-established processes, smaller organisations can allow workers to take risks (Rottwilm 2014, p. 7). In comparison, smaller organisations can be more efficient, as they do not have the layers of management needed in larger organisations. However, smaller staff sizes mean responsibilities and labour increase. Legacy media organisations such as *The Age* tend to be part of much larger media 'stables' with slower and centralised decision-making processes, and many more stakeholders in the process of change. Nikki Usher's (2014) ethnographic profile of *The New York Times'* move to digital production suggested similar lumbering towards change; while journalists grappled with a number of competing interests between traditional journalism ideology and new communication environments empowered by online and social media, the speed of change in the overall organisational structure both encouraged and stifled innovation in news production.

These economic and managerial concerns with organisational success indicate that there is a difference between what a successful 'commercial organisation' looks like compared with a successful 'journalism organisation'. This difference points to two very different organisational considerations—firstly, the way the structure of the organisation and its profit-making opportunities are positioned, and secondly, the way the culture of the newsroom and relations between various news stakeholders contribute to editorial success. What can be compared more readily are the concrete examples of divergence in the organisational approach to social media use in the newsroom, and the strategies, policies and roles that respond to this new editorial context for news organisations. Moving away from trying to find single elements that indicate a news organisation's successful transition into digital, online and social media-enabled news environments enables a stronger focus on newsroom relations, and the interlinked elements of strategy, policy, employee roles and professional ideologies that work together to create a successful newsroom (Harper 2010).

Journalism Practice in the Social Media-Enabled Newsroom

Social media environments have pushed news media organisations, both established and new, to think more carefully about production and distribution of content. Similarly, the growing importance of social media's role as an intermediary for news distribution means that, increasingly, referral traffic to news sites comes from *Facebook* or search engines. Most news organisations have responded to these changes by investing heavily in search engine optimisation, as well as readership analytics. The availability and relatively low cost of these tools and associated algorithmic manipulation of the prominence of news (see Chap. 5) have also impacted on the structure, policies and labour expectations of editors, managers and journalists. Research, planning and strategy about what the news audience looks like, and what information they need at any one time is now a predominant concern of news organisations. This focus on distributed dissemination of news content means it is the 'findability' and 'shareability' of news that is often most commercially valuable to news organisations. This has sometimes meant that organisational focus has moved away from local and general news to increasingly automated and aggregated content or wire and syndication services.

An overreliance on aggregated content, celebrity news and 'click bait' have been some of the negative consequences of news organisations competing with online publications. Journalists who have worked for *The Age*, for example, have suggested that although their commitment to the public service imperative of news has not changed, the commercial imperatives for 'hits' on their stories has influenced their practice (R. Myer, personal communication, 31 March 2017; L. Schwartz, personal communication, 23 March 2017). Managerial encouragement to write shorter articles for online publication, as well as the speed required to produce news in a 24-hour newsroom, have been central to concerns about declining quality in news organisations. Former *Age* journalist Rod Myer (personal communication, 31 March 2017) suggests that in post-online, social media-enabled newsrooms, where cutbacks and redundancies have created lean newsrooms focussed on ensuring engagement with branded news content, there have been a number of changes to editorial expectations. In this environment, journalists are constantly under pressure to keep up with the speed of online news distribution: 'journalists are writing non-stop to have the news out when it happens, so you might have three to four deadlines per day and on big stories, you might be updating throughout the day. The internet never sleeps so the newspaper never goes to bed' (R. Myer, personal communication, 31 March 2017). This speed coupled with the commercial imperatives of ensuring content is click-worthy has a number of impacts on everyday journalism, especially on a journalist's ideologically prized ability to 'sniff out a good story' (R. Myer, personal communication, 31 March 2017).

One of the more problematic issues concerning the focus on commercial aspects of news sharing is the creation of a culture of 'perverse incentives' in the newsroom. Journalists report that they now find it harder to create news stories to improve public dialogue because their once-autonomous news sense is stymied by expectations that they will write what potential audiences might click on, rather than what is needed for the public record (R. Myer, personal communication, 31 March 2017). This is, of course, an ideological argument based on the discursive construction of a journalist's sole authority to represent the news. However, overreliance on the commercial imperatives of news has been shown to cause reputational damage to a news organisation over time. For example, *BuzzFeed* has been repeatedly criticised for using material from other media organisations without attribution (Bump 2013) and faced subsequent law suits over alleged copyright infringement. Since then, the company has been trying to change its reputation as a 'listicle' site, with investments in serious news, but has nonetheless courted controversy about unethical journalistic practices. Most recently, *BuzzFeed* published an unverified dossier of information about US President Donald Trump's alleged relationship with Russia (Gezari 2017).

More importantly, commercial reliance on audience preference has a chilling effect on journalist's confidence that their news organisation will publish less click-worthy, but nonetheless important, news content (R. Myer, personal communication, 31 March 2017). This creates a culture of perverse incentives in the newsroom; that is, the incentive to produce commercially viable news products generates adverse reputational consequences due to the journalists' actions. Journalists become incentivised to produce news that audiences will readily click onto, because this may provide professional kudos and increased popularity of their online content. This might be overlaid with time and resource pressures to produce particular kinds of journalism and other professional pressures to ensure their individual popularity on social media. Focussing solely on the popularity of content, however, may diminish the editorial quality of news work and the reputation of the associated news organisation, as well as fuelling distrust of professional journalism practices by audiences.

The issue of perverse incentives appears to stem from the short-term logic of the opportunities provided by social media and search intermediaries to reach increasingly distributed audiences (Nielsen and Ganter 2017). This creates a fear of missing the potential online influence and popularity that comes with large-scale audience engagement with news products. However, this is framed by a lack of real understanding of what the rewards of this influence will actually be and, more broadly, how this might regulate or govern news production. Thus, perverse incentives within journalistic practice are structured by the paradoxical fear of both 'missing out' and losing control; while most journalists and their news organisations are keen to partake in the economies of online popularity, giving up editorial control as a result of this reliance on intermediary media organisations creates tensions in the newsroom.

Reliance on optimisation for sharing and trending on social media has altered the types of roles needed in news organisations, as well as their skill sets and professional ideologies. Extending from this, the structures, role descriptions and strategic focuses of news production are changing. Nielsen and Schrøder (2014) suggest that we are moving from the traditional 'news cycle' produced by journalists, editors and their choice of sources to an 'information cycle': a complex series of relations that integrates audiences with organisational processes of news production. New social media-focussed roles are also crucial to mapping the development of both organisational structures and work routines, foregrounding processes and practices alongside affordances, consolidation of new skills, as well as organisational diversification (McCosker 2017).

Management of the Social Media Newsroom—New Roles, New Cultures

While the organisational response to the introduction of social media as a news production and distribution tool has had many effects on journalistic practice, these changes have also required the development of different editorial strategies, policies and job functions in the newsroom. An important, but often unacknowledged, change that has taken place in the social media-enabled newsroom is the new relationships between different management, editorial, journalistic and multimedia workers in the newsroom. Journalists have always been represented as having a measure of autonomy in the newsroom; other than the provision made for editors to assign journalists to particular stories, the sourcing, investigation and approach to creating a news story has mostly been represented as an individual effort. What journalists have never been able to control, however, is the structure, resourcing and overall strategy of the organisation they work for; their labour, no matter how autonomous, is shaped by the structure of their news organisation.

The new economic conditions of producing journalism have changed roles and work conditions. The advent of extreme job losses and cost-cutting exercises in legacy mainstream media has created a number of different work arrangements for journalists—most new recruits are expected to be web and multimedia-savvy and to be able to file for several platforms during their work day. Increasing use of social media, both by organisations and by individual journalists, has also added a promotional character to their role (Rottwilm 2014, p. 3). This has meant that journalists are expected to 'brand' or market themselves as individual professionals, primarily using social media as the platform for increasing their online popularity, and that, by extension, organisations might benefit from this online influence (see Chap. 6).

Some research is beginning to illustrate how social media technologies are changing the structure of news organisations, especially in the creation of new social media and technology-focussed roles and the expansion of the commercial uses of social media within organisations (Treem and Leonardi 2013). Nielsen (2012), for example, has suggested that in news organisations it is technologists that have had an active role in the transition of legacy newsrooms into online and social media-enabled work spaces. Nielsen's (2012) ethnographic work showed that while many news organisations were focussed on the adoption of the similar types of online technologies, the relations between stakeholders in the newsroom determined the different ways these technologies were utilised. The relations between these stakeholders influence the ways new processes, policies and work routines shape organisational use of social media's affordances (Raviola 2012). To avoid the kind of determinism that suggests technological change as the main influence on journalistic practice, the use of those technologies in relation to other stakeholders, as well as organisational structures and professional ideologies, must be considered. Each aspect will have an influence, both positive and negative, on the newsroom's adoption of social media. For example, journalistic and editorial-focussed staff might define the use of social media through particular professional and editorial frameworks (Nielsen 2012). However, management and executive staff might consider the reputational and commercial potential of social media. Technologically focussed staff might have a further concern for social media's specific usability. The way social media is adopted into the daily routines of journalists and newsrooms will vary, depending on the definitions ascribed to these new roles; the way these new roles are adopted and relate to other stakeholders will also determine their success. While the potential for innovation is important, it also needs to be balanced with management of new work roles and practices that may add complexity to relations in the newsroom (Westlund 2011).

Many researchers (Bossio and Sacco 2016; Holton and Molyneux 2015; Gleason 2010) have noted the increasing appearance of social media editors and community managers in the newsroom of legacy, digital and online-only media organisations. These are often full-time staff members with duties and jurisdiction similar to an editor, but whose roles are completely dedicated to the use of social media tools for both editorial and promotional production of news. These social media staff are often junior, filling newly created positions with the expectation that they will innovate in the role (McCosker 2017). They do not always have journalism expertise, but may also come from communications or marketing backgrounds. Social media managers often facilitate use of multiple social media accounts on various platforms and are integral to determining what platforms are used and for what purpose, how content on each platform should be developed and strategically utilised, and how other workers in the organisation should engage with social media on personal and professional accounts. While the role of the social media manager is particularly diverse, social media strategy and policy, content development and data analysis are key. Within news organisations, these considerations are complicated by the editorial concerns of the newsroom, as well as the broader professional ideology that news serves a social function of generating public information and discourse.

In research conducted into social media integration in Australian newsrooms, Sacco and Bossio (2017) found that there was some variation in the ways editorial and management staff attempted to integrate social media use in the newsroom, including hiring of new staff, social media training and implementation of new policies and guidelines—or a combination of these techniques. This variation often depended on the size of the organisation, the relationships between different newsroom workers and, importantly, the way the social media manager viewed their own role. Some social media managers took an editorial approach to their role, overseeing the organisational use of social media, and working with journalists to produce content on their individual accounts. Others took more of a managerial approach, ensuring that journalistic practices and commercial interests were aligned. Despite these differences in the framing of their role, most understood their role as multifaceted, describing both a journalistic and management component to their daily duties (Sacco and Bossio 2017).

Some news organisations also create formal policies and training mechanisms to guide the editorial and promotional use of social media in the newsroom, in conjunction with (or instead of) hiring social media management staff. Social media policy or guidelines can be defined in this regard as the formalisation of organisational jurisdiction over the conduct of journalists and other editorial staff in the use of social media for news production, dissemination and promotion. The use of social media policies and guidelines centres on the reputation of either the journalist or the media organisation—that is, ensuring individual content posted on social media meets with the interests of the media organisation overall (see Chap. 6 for further discussion of social media policy use by journalists). The structure of these policies and their implementation impacts the utility of social media in the newsroom; journalists negotiate the 'rules' governing social media use when deciding whether social media is used as an editorial or a promotional tool on behalf of their organisation or individual professional goals.

Similarly, these new roles and guidelines create new work practices that develop the skills and professional frameworks needed to practise as a journalist in a social media-enabled newsroom. Some of these practices are positive, including increased public engagement and more opportunities to source varied viewpoints and experience through links made on social media. However, employment precariousness and increased labour have also been part of the introduction of social media to the newsroom. For example, Terranova (2004) has suggested the difficulties associated with social media's 'affective labour'; the work of attempting to affect audience reaction and engagement with particular media products, including news. The use of social media to promote news stories using appeals to everyday relevance and emotion is now often part of a journalist's labour—a sometimes overwhelming process of constant social media participation, distribution and engagement. These professional forms of engagement often seep into personal time, where journalists concerned to promote themselves, their work and their organisation, find themselves constantly checking and updating social media platforms (see Chap. 6). It is not just journalists who feel this pressure—social media strategists, community managers and moderators working within the newsroom are also expected to address online abuse and brand management, as well as the guidance of individual journalistic use of social media. As McCosker (2017) suggests, these demands on a workforce to participate on social media on behalf of an organisation are often time-consuming, difficult and emotionally draining, raising questions about how traditional management structures might need to develop to accommodate these new communication environments.

These changes to the production and distribution of news are obvious to anyone walking into *The Age* newsroom today. The newsroom is dominated by open-plan spaces, with 'doughnut shaped' desks to ensure interaction between online, video, audio and newspaper production staff. As well as traditional journalists, there are staff dedicated to digital content, video, streaming and social media. Nonetheless, all these staff are incredibly time-poor, the consequence of a number of staff cuts in the newsroom (More job cuts, 2017). In 2011, *Fairfax* employed over 1000 journalists, subeditors and photographers, but this number is now reduced by more than half (Fairfax cuts 2017). Nonetheless, many of the newer investments in online journalism have been much more successful than initial publishing experiments; *The Age* has continually remained in the top ten most popular news sites in Australia and its stable mate, *The Sydney Morning Herald*, in the top five. However, the increasing centralisation of media content in Sydney as a result of staff cuts in 2011, as well as the prioritisation of online click bait, have had negative effects in recent times. In 2017, *Fairfax* announced that they would cut another 125 jobs from the newsroom, saving $30 million (Mason 2017). The introduction of *The Guardian* to Australia and its heavy investment in local journalism and social media referrals have meant that *The Guardian* has overtaken *The Age* in reader popularity in just under four years. While *Fairfax*'s newspapers are still actually profitable, the organisation's overall revenue is falling at around 10% per year (Fairfax cuts 2017). This is due mostly to the gap between print and digital advertising, the latter bringing only a fraction of traditional advertising. While the job cuts will go ahead, Fairfax also recently reported a takeover bid by the American private equity firm *TPG* for $2.7 billion, though the company would break up the media organisation's assets, which include a television streaming company, local newspapers, radio stations and local media organisations in New Zealand (Silk 2017). Tellingly, *TPG* only saw value in *Fairfax*'s enormously profitable online real estate website, *Domain*—and their long-established and reputable metropolitan news organisations.

Of course, it is not just *Fairfax* bearing the brunt of harsh economic times; their largest Australian rival, *News Corp*, also recently announced large-scale staff cuts to save $40 million (Mason 2016). What is apparent is that these large-scale organisational changes impact the production of news—and many of these changes have been brought about by new online and social media-enabled news environments. Indeed, as news organisations were announcing cuts to ensure their long-term sustainability, *Facebook* announced its advertising revenues had increased by 51% worldwide (Frier 2017). These shifts in the wider media landscape reflect the changes occurring in individual journalism practice and in news organisations; journalists and legacy news organisations no longer enjoy the same autonomy and social authority in the public sphere to represent news and information. As the various affordances of communication technologies and their cultures have become more widely adopted, legacy news organisations and the traditional journalism practices they support have had to shift to accommodate new ways of producing and commercialising news. While individual journalists have not been able to escape the pressures of a shrinking traditional news industry, many have been able to integrate new, more collaborative and transparent forms of reportage into their practice. Similarly, while some journalists have often been somewhat ambivalent or even derisive of many of the new processes, policies and commercial strategies imposed on their practice, some have also worked with new multimedia, technical and social media-focussed managers to transition into new communications environments.

Conclusion

In this chapter, I have argued that news organisations and their management and production structures are important contributors to how journalists and journalism develop in the light of the various social, cultural and technical changes brought forth by social media communication. This is evident from the new roles and organisational structures that can be seen either to innovate with, or buttress against, the changes social media capacities bring to individual practitioners and across organisations. These changes are negotiated by individual practitioners, but are framed by the economic, strategic and employment roles and policy considerations structured within news media organisations. While new digital and online capabilities have fundamentally disrupted both the business model and production processes within the newsroom, social media capabilities have extended these changes into the distribution and promotional potential of news. This has influenced new communication cultures between journalists and audiences, as well as new relationships between journalists and other stakeholders in the newsroom. It is often these new relationships that contribute to the success of social media processes in the newsroom; just as individual journalistic practices have changed to incorporate collaboration and transparency, so too have organisational structures changed to allow a number of different skill sets to contribute to everyday journalism. These changes have a number of different effects, both positive and negative, on individual journalists and media organisations more broadly. In the next chapter, we continue the focus on social media's impacts on journalism organisations by exploring the organisational transition of the journalistic distribution of news on social media. Organisations transitioning into the prioritisation of social media news distribution and audience engagement are utilising processes of news production, distribution and consumption that are more collaborative, distributed and, increasingly, much more complex. Chap. 5 illustrates this complexity by describing the effects of opening up organisational processes to social media optimisation and algorithmic prioritisation.

References

ABC defends Four Corners report criticised by Nauru Government as 'biased political propaganda'. (2016, October 18). *ABC News.* Retrieved from http://www.abc.net.au/news/2016-10-18/nauru-dismisses-four-corners-report-biased-political-propoganda/7941964.

Bennett, L. (2016, September 23). Fairfax brings podcasts to newsroom with investigative series inspired by serial. *AdNews.* Retrieved from http://www.adnews.com.au/news/fairfax-brings-podcasts-to-newsroom-with-investigative-series-inspired-by-serial.

Bossio, D., & Sacco, V. (2016). Don't tweet this! How journalists and media organisations negotiate tensions emerging from the implementation of social media policy in newsrooms. *Digital Journalism, 5*(2), 177–193.

Bump, P. (2013, March 8). BuzzFeed's 'Happiest Facts of All Time' were mostly Plagiarized from Reddit. *The Atlantic.* Retrieved from https://www.theatlantic.com/business/archive/2013/03/buzzfeeds-happiest-facts-all-time-were-mostly-plagiarized-reddit/317576/.

Carson, A. (2015). Behind the newspaper paywall—lessons in charging for online content: A comparative analysis of why Australian newspapers are stuck in the purgatorial space between digital and print. *Media, Culture and Society, 37*(7), 1022–1041.

Edmonds, R. (2016, January 28). Newspapers aren't dying as fast as you think. *Poynter*. Retrieved from http://www.poynter.org/2016/just-how-alarming-are-newspaper-circulation-declines/393490/.

f2 Changes name to Fairfax Digital. (2004, August 2). *The Sydney Morning Herald*. Retrieved from http://www.smh.com.au/articles/2004/08/02/1091298616152.html.

Fairfax cuts hit hard. (2017, May 8). *Media Watch*. Retrieved from http://www.abc.net.au/mediawatch/transcripts/s4665341.htm.

Frew, W. (2003, September 30). Fairfax makes friendly bid for Text Media. *The Age*. Retrieved from http://www.theage.com.au/articles/2003/09/29/1064819870897.html.

Frier, S. (2017, February 2). Facebook sales top estimates on mobile ad gains. The *Sydney Morning Herald*. Retrieved from http://www.smh.com.au/technology/technology-news/facebook-sales-top-estimates-on-mobile-ad-gains-20170201-gu3oh3.html.

Gezari, V. M. (2017, January 11). BuzzFeed was right to publish Trump-Russia files. *Columbia Journalism Review*. Retrieved from http://www.cjr.org/criticism/buzzfeed_trump_russia_memos.php.

Gleason, S. (2010). Harnessing social media: News outlets are assigning staffers to focus on networking. *American Journalism Review, 32*(1), 6.

Global Entertainment and Media outlook. (2016). *PricewaterhouseCoopers Research*. Retrieved from http://www.pwc.com/gx/en/industries/entertainment-media/outlook/segment-insights/newspaper-publishing.html.

Harper, R. (2010). The social media revolution: Exploring the impact on journalism and news media organisations. *Inquiries Journal, 2*(3). Retrieved from http://www.inquiriesjournal.com/articles/202/the-social-media-revolution-exploring-the-impact-on-journalism-and-news-media-organisations.

Holton, A. E., & Molyneux, L. (2015). Identity lost? The personal impact of brand journalism. *Journalism*. http://doi.org/10.1177/1464884915608816.

Johnston, E. (2013, December 5). Fairfax sells Stayz accommodation website for $220 million to HomeAway. *The Sydney Morning Herald*. Retrieved from http://www.smh.com.au/business/fairfax-sells-stayz-accommodation-website-for-220m-tohomeaway-20131204-2yr41.html.

Knott, M. (2016, October 19). 'No evidence' for bias claims: ABC fires back at critics of Four Corners program on Nauru. *The Sydney Morning Herald*. Retrieved from www.smh.com.au/federal-politics/political-news/no-evidence-for-bias-claims-abc-fires-back-at-critics-of-four-corners-program-on-nauru-20161019.

Koziol, M. (2016, October 16). 'An embarrassment to journalism': Nauru government attacks 'racist' ABC over refugee report. *The Age*. Retrieved from http://www.smh.com.au/federal-politics/political-news/an-embarrassment-

to-journalism-nauru-government-attacks-racist-abc-over-refugee-report-20161017-gs4l8r.html.
Küng, L. (2015). *Innovators in Digital News*. London: I.B Tauris.
Levy, D., & Picard, R. G. (2011). *Is there a better structure for news providers? The potential in charitable and trust ownership*. Oxford: Reuters Institute for the study of Journalism.
Long, S. (2002, September 9). Fairfax posts low returns. *PM ABC*. Retrieved from http://www.abc.net.au/pm/stories/s671140.htm.
Lowe, S. (2002, April 5). LookSmart and f2 attempt to boost their strike rates. *The Sydney Morning Herald*. Retrieved from http://www.smh.com.au/articles/2002/04/04/1017206242172.html.
Mason, M. (2016, November 8). News Corp Australia to cut 40 million in costs including jobs. *The Australian Financial Review*. Retrieved from http://www.afr.com/business/media-and-marketing/publishing/news-corp-australia-to-cut-40-million-in-costs-including-jobs-20161108-gskbne.
Mason, M. (2017, May 7). Fairfax Media outlines 30 million in cost saving including staff cuts. *The Sydney Morning Herald*. Retrieved from http://www.smh.com.au/business/media-and-marketing/fairfax-media-outlines-30-million-in-cost-savings-including-staff-cuts-20170503-gvxuyd.html.
McCosker, A. (2017). Social media work: Reshaping organisational communications, extracting digital value. *Media International Australia*. Retrieved from http://journals.sagepub.com/doi/full/10.1177/1329878X17693702.
Meade, A. (2014, January 30). The Global Mail to close less than two years after its launch. *The Guardian*. Retrieved from https://www.theguardian.com/media/2014/jan/30/global-mail-website-to-close.
More job cuts looming for The Age publisher Fairfax media in $30 million savings push. (2017, April 5) Herald Sun. Retrieved from http://www.heraldsun.com.au/business/more-job-cuts-looming-for-the-age-publisher-fairfax-media-in-30m-savings-push/news-story/709325b10d8a138b741891923609c1a8.
Newman, N. (2016). Digital Media Report 2016. *Reuters Institute for the study of Journalism*. Retrieved from http://digitalnewsreport.org/survey/2016/overview-key-findings-2016/.
Nielsen, R. K. (2012). How newspapers began to blog: Recognizing the role of technologists in old media organisations' development of new media technologies. *Information, Communication & Society, 15*(6). Retrieved from http://www.tandfonline.com/doi/abs/10.1080/1369118X.2012.694898.
Nielsen, R. K., & Schrøder, C. K. (2014). The relative importance of social media for accessing, finding, and engaging with news: An eight-country cross-media comparison. *Digital Journalism, 2*(4), 472–479.
Nielsen, R. K., & Ganter, S. A. (2017). Dealing with digital intermediaries: A case study of the relations between publishers and platforms. *New*

Media and Society. Retrieved from http://journals.sagepub.com/eprint/dxNzFHygAIRHviKP9MFg/full.

Picard, R. G. (2010). *Value Creation and the future of news organisations: Why and how journalism must change to remain relevant in the 21st century*. Lisbon: Media XXI.

Picard, R. G. (2014). Twilight or New Dawn of Journalism: Evidence from a changing news ecosystem. *Journalism Studies, 15*(5), 500–510.

Raviola, E. (2012). Exploring organisational framings: Journalism and business management in newspaper organisations. *Information, Communication & Society, 15*(6). Retrieved from http://www.tandfonline.com/doi/abs/10.1080/1369118X.2012.696273.

Rottwilm, P. (2014, August). The future of journalistic work: Its future and implications. *Reuters Institute for the Study of Journalism*. Retrieved from https://reutersinstitute.politics.ox.ac.uk/sites/default/files/The%20Future%20of%20Journalistic%20Work%20%20Its%20Changing%20Nature%20and%20Implications.pdf.

Sacco, V., & Bossio, D. (2017). Don't tweet this! How journalists and media organisations negotiate tensions emerging from the implementation of social media policy in newsrooms. *Digital Journalism, 5*(2), 177–193.

Silk, M. (2017, May 8). Fairfax Media in $2.2 billion buyout talks with overseas consortium. *News.com*. Retrieved from http://www.news.com.au/finance/business/media/fairfax-media-in-22-billion-buyout-talks-with-overseas-consortium/newsstory/e9ca4c42b4d53221419d63565e28cec9.

Simons, M. (2007). *The content makers: Understanding the media in Australia*. Australia: Penguin.

Statement from the Government of Nauru. (2016, October 17). *Nauru-News.com*. http://www.nauru-news.com/single-post/2016/10/18/Statement-from-the-Government-of-Nauru-%E2%80%93-Re-Four-Corners-Oct-17-2016.

Terranova, T. (2004). *Network culture: Politics for the information age*. London: Pluto Press.

Tiffen, R. (2010). Changes in Australian newspapers 1956–2006. *Journalism Practice, 4*(3), 345–359.

Treem, J. W., & Leonardi, P. M. (2013). Social media use in organisations: Exploring the affordances of visibility, editability, persistence, and association. *Annals of the International Communication Association, 36*, 143–189.

Usher, N. (2014). *Making news at the New York Times*. USA: University of Michigan Press.

Westlund, O. (2011). *Cross-Media news work—Sensemaking of the mobile media (r)evolution*. Gothenburg: JMG Book Series No. 64.

Whitmont, D., & Harley, W. (2016, October 24). The Forgotten Children. *Four Corners.* Retrieved from www.abc.net.au/4corners/stories/2016/10/17/4556062.

Zion, L., Dodd, A., Sherwood, M., O'Donnell, P., Marjoribanks, T., & Ricketson, M. (2016). Working for less: The aftermath for journalists made redundant in Australian between 2012 and 2014. *Communication Research and Practice, 2*(2), 117–136.

CHAPTER 5

Big Data, Algorithms and the Metrics of Social Media News

On 23 June 2016, Britain voted in a new political reality—a reality that many politicians and media pundits had previously said would never happen (Ten Predictions 2016; Jack 2016b). When Prime Minister David Cameron promised in the 2015 election campaign that he would hold a referendum to re-negotiate European Union (EU) membership if the Conservative Party won a parliamentary majority at the general election, media commentary suggested it was simply a way to appease voter sentiment, rather than a true commitment to change. When the Conservatives won the majority in the House of Commons in May, Cameron proposed to hold a single-question 'In–Out' referendum after negotiating a new deal for Britain in the EU. Still, major news outlets suggested the 'Brexit' vote would come to naught (The hard-headed 2016). On the day of the referendum, as British votes for what had been reported as almost impossible just days before began to amass, deep shock was evident in the tone of the nation's mainstream media. Brexit was a reality. Data about the spread of votes suggested that while London overwhelmingly voted 'In', large parts of the north of England—though not Scotland—voted 'Out'. The media soul-searching began. How did journalists get the mood of the north of England so wrong?

In the days after the referendum, an 'elitist' news media was blamed for misunderstanding the extent of ill-will towards the EU in northern England (Jack 2016a, b; Perraudin 2016). This claim of media elitism would similarly be used against US journalists after Donald Trump swept

D. Bossio, *Journalism and Social Media*,
DOI 10.1007/978-3-319-65472-0_5

into the White House in 2016 (see Chap. 7). Both political campaigners and news media used a number of different ways to influence public dialogue about Brexit, with varying degrees of success. What became apparent after the referendum was that some campaigners for the 'Leave' vote had successfully used social media to influence voters (Kanter 2017). In Chap. 3, the heterogeneity of audiences and their media consumption habits were discussed; social media use by audiences was seen to empower new voices in the public sphere and increase opportunities for engagement and collaboration in the news agenda. In this chapter, I extend this focus to illustrate how organisational use of the data-driven and algorithmic characteristics of social media also attempt to influence audience news consumption and, therefore, public dialogue. The Brexit referendum showed that the heterogeneity of social media spaces, their languages and distribution methods all affect the circulation of news, information and opinion. Importantly, however, this heterogeneity also extended to other stakeholders invested in a particular media representation of Brexit, such as major and emerging political parties, community movements and individual political activists. These stakeholders used social media platforms to attempt to circumvent mainstream news representations of the vote. Thus, in understanding the transition to data and algorithmic journalism, we must 'decentralise' the journalist's role in news and information. Instead, the processes of news production, distribution and consumption are now collaborative, distributed and increasingly complex and, thus, open to an increasing number of influences on public dialogue.

In recent decades, the proliferation and use of data across industries has expanded exponentially. According to *IBM*, one billion gigabytes of data were generated every day in 2012, and this amount of created data has at least doubled every two years since (Bringing Big Data 2017). The use and management of data has enormous potential to influence most spheres of public and private life, though this brings as many issues as it does opportunities (Chen et al. 2014, p. 171). In the context of journalism, media and academic attention has begun to focus on the collection, organisation and use of data in reportage (Lewis 2015, p. 322). However, the number of different uses of data, both in an individual journalistic context, as well as a more commercially focussed organisational context, coupled with the related use of algorithms and social media analysis, has meant that discussion has sometimes become both overwhelming and unclear. Subsequently, the new skill sets, organisational processes and the overall institutional frameworks needed for understanding the role of data, computation and social media algorithms in journalism have not always been consistently applied (Lewis 2015, p. 322).

This chapter firstly provides an outline of the roles of data in journalism, from its beginnings in computer-assisted reporting (CAR) to the more recent discussion of the use of social media analytics and algorithms in journalism. In doing so, this chapter illustrates that the organisation, management and presentation of various forms of data and algorithmic information have become, and will continue to be, an increasingly important part of individual and organisational journalistic practice. Computational and data journalism have long been acknowledged, if not always well utilised, as important parts of journalism in the public interest. Indeed, media-savvy journalists have worked both independently and in collaboration with others to use data within everyday reportage, especially in the increasing use of data visualisation. However, this chapter argues that the new challenge for journalism is the increasingly savvy manipulation by other political stakeholders of social media algorithms, especially those that focus on prioritisation and filtering of news to influence audience consumption habits. While news organisations are increasingly pushing content out through a number of social media platforms to improve the number of views of news content, they are competing with other stakeholders hoping to influence the way news discourses are represented. Using a media analysis of the Brexit vote as a case study, this chapter suggests that rapid developments in the use and distribution of data create both challenges and opportunities for journalism, especially in the intervention into audience data and manipulation of algorithms structuring information reach and popularity.

Data and the Context for Journalism

As shock at the referendum's 'Leave' result began to register internationally, many news organisations turned to the data that would best illustrate voter sentiment across Britain. Media reportage in the days after the Brexit vote illustrated a number of different journalistic uses of social media and data. Journalists used data as a tool for reportage and news organisations used data to analyse the popularity of their content and its distribution. Voter registration numbers, local turnout data and, of course, vote counts were mapped and distributed as the votes came in, and in the subsequent analysis of the referendum results (EU Referendum 2016). Interactive maps of Britain, as well as graphs indicating votes by age, income and ethnicity all showed how the 'Leave' campaign had triumphed, albeit by a very small majority. While technologists, statisticians and journalists were crunching the voter data, news organisations were also analysing data—their online and social media traffic. Indeed, the audience traffic for EU referendum news created new web records (Sweney 2016). For example, on the day of the referendum, *The Guardian* recorded the most traffic in its online history, with 17 million unique browsers and 77 million page views, overtaking the *Mail Online*, the most-viewed English-language news website in the world (Sweney 2016). These different representations suggest that there are many different uses of data in journalism, and these uses are evolving as journalists become more 'data-savvy'.

Data is described in computing as information that has been translated into a digital binary form so it is easier for a computer to process. In recent times, online and social media use has meant that data has been a lot easier to generate and issues concerning the collection and management of massive data emerging from public and private sources have emerged (Chen et al. 2014, p. 171). Social media, especially, has contributed to an explosion of data production, including textual data, such as tweets and comments, network data, such as *Twitter* followers, and data concerning an individual's location, links, likes, shares and views. 'Big' data, compared with traditional sets of data, is defined as much larger amounts of generally unstructured data that needs more time for processing and analysis (Chen et al. 2014, p. 171). Journalism scholars have been interested in big data in particular as part of new journalistic methods of gaining, analysing and presenting news (Coddington 2015), as well as processes of automation and computation in the production of news (Carlson 2015). While algorithms have been discussed in the context of data journalism, they differ from data; algorithms are the sets of rules for the sequence of actions that must be taken to process data, perform calculations or automate a decision-making process. Thus, data-driven journalism might consider how massive data sets can be managed to represent coherent analysis and represent this in news stories, while algorithmic journalism might consider what values are more powerful to audiences online and then set rules in the analysis of data that prioritise those values.

A recent example of both data and algorithmic journalism is the explosive revelations contained in data analysis of the so-called 'Panama Papers'. The Panama Papers are a series of news stories stemming from the leak, by an anonymous source, of 11.5 million files from the offshore law firm, *Mossack Fonseca*. The files were sent to the German newspaper *Süddeutsche Zeitung*, which then shared them with the *International Consortium of Investigative Journalists* (*ICIJ*). The *ICIJ* then assisted in creating a collaborative journalism project between international news organisations to mine the data for potential news stories (Harding 2016). Over 100 news organisations simultaneously released news stories stemming from almost 2.6 terabytes of data, the biggest single leak of data in news history (Harding 2016). More than 400 journalists worked for over a year to comb through 4.8 million emails, 3 million database files and 2.1 million other documents (Greenberg 2016). Amongst the stories were revelations that the Icelandic Prime Minister had not disclosed his ownership of a stake in several Icelandic banks, and that Russian President Vladimir Putin had hidden almost $2 billion in the bank accounts of family members and friends (Henley 2016; Harding 2016).

The *ICIJ* managed the journalistic process through collaborative use of both data and algorithmic processes. Firstly, the organisation worked with web developers to create a collaborative online space with a two-factor, authentication-protected search engine that was shared between journalists in different countries via a URL sent by encrypted email (Greenberg 2016). For the subsequent analysis of the files, the *ICIJ* worked with a software company to create the algorithms that would allow the data to be sorted, organised and, subsequently, to be searchable (Greenberg 2016). Optical character recognition was used to transform the data into text that could be searched and then inserted into a database (Burgess 2016). Once the information had been indexed in the database, algorithms were programmed to prioritise specific links, and these automated processes worked in conjunction with data that journalists manually created, such as lists of important politicians or international criminals (Burgess 2016). The publications stemming from the Panama Papers thus show that modern data journalism is not simply the interpretation of data into graphs or narrative format, but also methodologies for computation and automation of reportage practices (Lewis 2015, p. 323). These methodologies are not necessarily journalist-led; rather, journalists are working collaboratively with different media stakeholders, such as web developers and programmers, for the purpose of sourcing and analysing news. Thus, while there are a number of potential benefits for creation of data-driven and algorithmic news processes, there are also large-scale disruptions to journalistic labour and social authority that should also be considered (see Carlson 2015).

Journalism's Turn to Computation and Data

While data-driven and algorithmic journalism may seem 'new', the turn towards CAR has been developing over many years. In 1967, Philip Meyer won a Pulitzer Prize for his innovative use of an IBM personal computer to survey and profile rioters in the 1967 Detroit Riots (Meyer 2011). The use of computing-inspired social science methods for reportage was seen as innovative, and Meyer subsequently published a book on this methodology (Meyer 1979). During the mid to late 1980s, Meyer promoted the use of computing as a tool to facilitate survey and other sociological methods for journalism. As CAR gained more attention from journalists and scholars, journalists used computer-based tools like spreadsheets, databases and collections of text-based reports to investigate large-scale political and social issues. Despite being the focus of much discussion in the media and academia, and producing some impressive reporting and analysis, CAR was not quickly adopted as a mainstream journalism tool. While some newsrooms were slow to invest in computing technologies and training, journalists themselves were often reluctant to add the new techniques to their practice.

Nonetheless, some computational skills have been integrated into journalism practice, with data mining, statistical analysis and data visualisation now seen as standard journalism practices. Coddington (2015, p. 334) suggests that CAR's social science methodologies, and the statistical and computer-based research skills it embodies, formed the basis for the data-driven journalism that has emerged as a 'quantitative turn' in journalism practice. For example, in 2004, *The Oregonian*, led by Steve Suo, published a series of investigative journalism articles showing that the US Congress and its Drug Enforcement Administration could have stopped methamphetamine growth across the West during the 1990s. Using CAR methods, journalists examined reports of DEA drug seizures, drug shipments, seizures, and congressional records. This allowed the newspaper to conclude that methamphetamine importation could have been controlled because its production requires chemicals produced by only a handful of factories worldwide (see Interview 2005).

Journalists could evidence this by using reports that showed two prior clampdowns and subsequent chemical shortages had seen meth addiction and related property crime fall. This series of articles shows how the quantitative turn in journalism is characterised by focus on both the methods of finding information, and subsequently, the methods of representing data in journalistic storytelling.

Newer forms of data and computational journalism have extended on traditional CAR by prioritising forms of collaboration and transparency in methodology, as well as processes of abstraction and automation in analysing and utilising information (Lewis 2015, p. 324). The social, cultural, and technological impacts of data abundance, both in terms of the variety of potential use for data representation and analysis, as well as the challenges and opportunities that these uses provide, are only growing as computing and software increases in capability (see Lewis and Westlund 2014, p. 447). These issues and opportunities have been seen in the inclusion of programming and data specialist roles and training within newsrooms, as well as the greater use of probability modelling, coding and interactivity in everyday journalism. This has, of course, raised questions about the role of journalists, as well as the kinds of labour a digital and social media-enabled newsroom might need now and in future.

Interactions between journalists and other media workers to facilitate new data-driven reporting methods have become important as openness, transparency and cross-field collaboration dominate digital, online and social media-enabled news environments. The traditional boundaries between journalism-focussed, technology and management roles are increasingly breaking down in these environments as new and legacy media organisations try to understand how to harness the value of different forms of data (see Chap. 4). The 2014 Carbon Emissions interactive produced for *The Guardian* (Carbon Emissions 2014) is a good example of how these new relationships work to produce journalism. The interactive shows a timeline of how the top 20 carbon-emitting nations have changed since the 1880s, the amount of carbon produced, and scenarios for cutting emissions. To produce this interactive, journalists at *The Guardian* collaborated with the *World Resources Institute* to research the story, and the web development company *Kiln* produced the story itself as an online interactive. As suggested in Chap. 2, traditional norms of journalism, such as autonomy, are transitioning into processes of collaboration and transparency and, thus, in digital environments, the journalist is no longer the centre of knowledge. In this example, journalists also works with other research experts to produce a story from data and other networked forms of information, while technologists and other media experts find the best way of representing the data in story form. *The Guardian's* Carbon Emissions interactive is an example of the kinds of new collaborations and storytelling that have emerged with the focus on data in journalism. However, this example still assumes the prioritisation of human-based journalism practices and interactions to find the story within data. While the professional ideologies that underpin CAR methodologies maintain the centrality of the journalist in finding the story within otherwise 'neutral' data sets (Parasie and Dagiral 2013, p. 859), more contemporary data journalism has disrupted these traditional journalistic boundaries. Indeed, newer uses of algorithmic and automated journalism prioritise human and machine-based interactions, and even limit the need for humans in data sourcing and analysis altogether.

From Data to Algorithmic Journalism

Algorithms are both the 'consequence and cause of the "big data" phenomenon' (Napoli 2014, p. 340). Where big data promised more possibilities for news stories within vast swathes of information waiting to be 'unlocked' by journalists, algorithms enable consistent analysis of this data, sometimes without the need for journalists. Algorithms are used in the process of journalism at several stages, including searching for and classifying information, manipulating distribution of news to particular audiences and even in the automation of news writing (see Anderson 2013; Carlson 2015). Further to this, the increasing use of social media in journalism has meant that social media algorithms and analytics have been increasingly important to understand the distribution and impact of news in various audience groups. Social media analytics are used predominantly by media organisations to extract insights about readership and distribution of news content through processing and analysis of social media data, such as shares, likes, tweets and links. This gives a representation of which news stories are being read and shared and the kinds of content that might dominate audience choice.

An algorithm's utility—and power—is in the different ways it can assert consistent rules. This power is used at both practitioner and organisational levels to influence reporting practices and audience engagement with news through programming processes of prioritisation, filtering and classification of news and information. For example, a news organisation might use a prioritisation algorithm to change the way news is seen online, determining what gets seen at the top of the news page. Thus, the algorithmic turn in news media production and consumption relates to its key function in assisting, but also regulating, the ways in which individual users navigate online and social media environments (Napoli 2014). Social media audiences now encounter algorithmic decisions made for them every day when they use search, recommendation, and content aggregation systems (Anderson 2006). Gillespie (2014) suggests that algorithms exist as a communication technology because they 'are caught up in and are influencing the ways in which we ratify knowledge for civic life' through the consistent suggestion and application of a mass understanding of likes and preferences. Thus, it is important to consider how algorithms prioritise and filter decisions about media consumption, how these interventions into news production and distribution are socially and politically structured and, finally, how those interventions by other media stakeholders can influence news communication processes.

News organisations and journalists have prioritised the need for algorithms in news production and distribution in different ways. The editorial use of algorithms to create consistent rules around analysis has been useful in investigative processes, though the increasing automation of journalism processes has brought up issues of employment precariousness. Similarly, automated processes of journalism have required consideration of the role of the journalist in the newsroom more broadly, especially, when it is important for a journalist to intervene in the analysis and production of news. Similarly, both editorial and strategic considerations have influenced use of algorithms in the newsroom. News organisations have hired technical specialists to program algorithms for editing, automating production and distribution of content, as well as aggregating content from other news sources (Dorr 2016). Further to this, news organisations have invested heavily in the analysis of news consumption data to analyse which news stories and journalists are most popular online and on social media, as well as tracking clicks, likes and shares. Thus, where the need and potential importance of a news story was once decided by editors using a subjective and ideological understanding of the public interest, data about audience news consumption makes public interest decisions much more precise—and popularity driven.

Nonetheless, both journalistic and algorithmic decision-making share similarities in that they both attempt to structure a kind of public logic; the assertion of algorithmic objectivity is represented in a similar way to the traditional norm of objectivity in journalism (see Chap. 2). As Gillespie (2014) suggests, 'Like search engines, journalists have developed tactics for determining what is most relevant, how to report it, and how to assure its relevance—a set of practices that are relatively invisible to their audience, that they admit are messier to deal with than they might appear, and that help set aside but do not eradicate value judgments and personal politics'. But the objectives of journalism and algorithms are not the same—journalists use objectivity as a kind of institutional promise of expertise to audiences, whereas algorithms suggest a machine-led neutrality that structures a kind of public. Gillespie (2014) suggests that providers of algorithmic services, such as search engines, are invested in the representation of algorithmic neutrality. Like journalism, the supposed neutrality of algorithms suggests their social and public good, legitimising many of their technical and commercial undertakings, against the messier and more subjective reality of algorithmic choices (Gillespie 2010).

Thus, two issues emerge with the increasingly strategic use of algorithms in journalism: firstly, the editorial influence that algorithmically determined 'popular' news stories have on the production values of journalism; and secondly, the unintended consequences of increasingly complex algorithms on the production and consumption of news on social media. Napoli (2014) suggests that algorithms are spawning mutual influence and reflexivity in algorithmically driven media consumption. That is, if particular algorithms emphasise the most seen, engaged with or popular content, only initially 'popular' content will continually be recommended, thus inhibiting less popular content from actually gaining any engagement. This embeds a set of market-driven 'value propositions' that are necessarily biased towards what a news organisation thinks will get the largest audience, as opposed to what might be in the public interest. This might also increase pressure on news organisations to gather more data to better utilise the processing capacity of the algorithms in which they have invested, bringing journalism further away from human processes of media production (Napoli 2014, p. 340).

Social media platforms themselves have particular algorithms that also affect the ways audiences receive and distribute news (see Chap. 7). Indeed, the frameworks set by algorithms have much more influence on what audiences see online and on social media, rather than human-centred editorial decision-making. However, the criteria determining these values and choices are not made public, especially by private organisations, and thus it is difficult to understand the influence that these values might have on news-making, or to adjust editorial decision-making accordingly (Diakopoulos 2015). The notion of platform politics (Gillespie 2010; Cheney-Lippold 2011) illustrates the way algorithmic decision-making and manipulation can structure public dialogue. In articulating its apparent neutrality, the public, commercial and social ramifications of algorithmic decision-making are obscured. However, both the network infrastructure of the Internet and the enthusiasm of public sharing, liking and content production of individual users have led to mass processing of information and the mechanical inferences of 'categories of identity on otherwise anonymous beings' (Cheney-Lippold 2011, p. 165). Where once journalists would appeal to a particular discursive construction of an audience that could be actively re-presented or challenged, Cheney-Lippold (2011, p. 165) argues that 'we are entering an online world where our identifications are largely made for us. A "new algorithmic identity" is situated at a distance from traditional liberal politics, removed from civil discourse via the proprietary nature of many algorithms while simultaneously enjoying an unprecedented ubiquity in its reach to surveil and record data about users'. Thus, social media platforms, through the collection of enormous amounts of data and the thousands of machine-led decisions that categorise it, are sociopolitical, in that they 'softly persuade users towards models of normalised behaviour and identity through the constant redefinition of categories of identity' (Cheney-Lippold 2011, p. 177). This is not to suggest that algorithms are deterministic of behaviour—rather, that they are relational, being enacted and stabilised by representations of their neutrality, but also open to the manipulation and re-interpretation by other stakeholders in the representation of public dialogue.

In this context, the design and programming of algorithms both enable and delimit the possibilities of communication in online and social media environments, and thus a journalist's ability to produce and distribute news. The growing complexity and commercial secrecy framing algorithmic influence, especially on social media, are important because it is these platforms that are now acting as news distributors—and where increasing numbers are finding out about news. A number of new ethical and political issues have emerged with the influence of algorithms on news, especially concerning their capacity to structure user behaviours and, by extension, news production decisions. Thus, algorithms are not merely a technical part of the news production process, but instead influence journalism through subjective decision-making shaped by social, organisational and institutional environments (Diakopoulos 2015). This can become problematic for institutional framing of journalism because algorithmic rules reinforce the market-based needs of news organisations, rather than the public interest values of traditional journalism (Tandoc and Thomas 2015).

Diakopoulos (2015) argues that the use of algorithms to create rules of content analysis and distribution raises questions about 'how decisions of inclusion and exclusion are made, what styles of reasoning are employed, whose values are embedded into the technology, and how they affect public understanding of complex issues'. That is, the use of data and associated algorithms is not 'neutral', but influenced by the various priorities of stakeholders in the news, whether they be news-focussed, or influenced by political, commercial or other interests. The complexity and broad use of algorithms makes it difficult to scrutinise whether they have been focussed on the editorial, business or strategic needs of a news organisation and it is thus difficult to account for potential 'algorithmic influences' on news production and distribution. Furthermore, while the influence exerted by the use of algorithms on news reception and distribution might be intentional, such as bias towards a news organisation's commercial interests, other impacts might be incidental, such as unintended discriminatory prioritisation on search engines (Miller 2015).

While economic and market-based influences on news production are hardly new issues for journalism, it is perhaps the complexity, dynamism and overall inscrutability of algorithms that are new considerations for practitioners and organisations. For example, one of the major ethical issues to emerge from algorithmic production of journalism is the 'unintended agency' that these automated processes take on over time. The sometimes discriminatory frameworks that underpin search and recommendation algorithms have been documented, as has the structuring influence of like algorithms on news distribution on social media (Hermida 2014, p. 61). Human agency is central to the ongoing development and modification of algorithmic journalism, but as these processes become more complex, they may also have unintended consequences. That is, algorithms are dynamic; as they are constantly adapted by different stakeholders and for different reasons, the potential for new and unintended potentiality also expands (Napoli 2014). For example, a journalist was allegedly able to find FBI Director James Comey's secret *Twitter* account in about four hours by exploiting recommendation algorithms on another platform (Feinberg 2017). The journalist found the account by finding Comey's son on *Instagram*; even though the account was locked, *Instagram*'s recommendation algorithms suggested other accounts the journalist might want to follow based on the follower list of the otherwise locked account. This list gave enough clues for the journalist to find Comey's possible *Instagram* account and, from there, deduce his profile name on other platforms.

The use of data and algorithms in journalism is underpinned by the fact that they are technically dynamic—their use will only increase in possibilities and complexity as technological function increases. This means that it will not necessarily be journalists who innovate the use of data and algorithmic journalism in future, but rather change will occur in collaboration with programmers and other technologists. Thus, new institutional understandings of journalism will not place journalists at its centre, but rather the collaborative work that is done to influence public dialogue will be key to understanding transitions in journalism. If the place of algorithms in public dialogue is not determined by the ideologies of journalism, the influence of other social, cultural and political stakeholders in the representation of news must also be considered, including their commercial and strategic function in regulating individual communication behaviours (Napoli 2014). Lewis and Usher (2013) have suggested new forms of collaboration and transparency across journalism roles means that journalists now act like 'knowledge managers' who work with a number of stakeholders to facilitate the research and analysis of information within a story.

While influence and control over news and information were once concerning effects of traditional news media ownership, the new complexity of media production and consumption and the number of stakeholders involved in processes of making and distributing news and information raises similar concerns about political, commercial and strategic influence on news and information on social media. The political implications of algorithmic functions cannot be ignored—especially the independent ability to affect the flow of news and information through intervention in these functions (Diakopoulos 2015). Recent political examples show that business and political stakeholders in media representation are well ahead of journalists in the understanding and manipulation of algorithms for commercial and political gain. The coverage of Brexit is one example where journalism has struggled to keep up with the pace of change in news reporting using social media.

Brexit Campaigners' Use of Social Media

News reporting about the Brexit campaign was perhaps an early example of how content on social media platforms could be manipulated to increase audience reach. While preliminary research (Deakon et al. 2016) showed that many of the mainstream news organisations in Britain did fairly report both sides of the argument, readership and circulation affected the distribution of more subjective or opinionated reportage in favour of the Leave campaign. A comparison of the total percentages of Remain to Leave news items in mainstream news organisations in Britain found 41% were pro-Remain and 59% were pro-Leave—a relatively balanced distribution. However, when considered in relation to the circulation numbers of individual news organisations, the gap widens to 18% pro-Remain and 82% pro-Leave, because many of the highest-circulating newspapers supported Brexit in news coverage (Deakon et al. 2016). Campaign organisations were also much more savvy about using social media platform algorithms to their strategic advantage. Similarly, while the audience reach and popularity of the news organisation had an enormous impact on the representation of pro-Leave and pro-Remain sentiment, some campaign groups were so strategic in their use of social media that their overall political popularity had no bearing on the audience reach of their message. Indeed, what has become increasingly clear in the analysis of both online traffic and audience reach of content is that, despite its popularity after the referendum, mainstream journalism was not relied upon by political stakeholders to report campaign messages, nor to authenticate or add credibility to a campaign message. Traditional interdependence between the political and the journalism spheres to provide understanding and analysis to the public was upended during Brexit and campaign use of social media instead prioritised unfiltered, direct messaging to potential voters. It was the Leave campaign that especially circumvented traditional news media and advertising coverage by using social media posting.

Marciano (2016) indicated that the two main pro- and anti-Brexit websites, *voteleavetakecontrol.org* and *strongerin.co.uk*, differed in prioritisation of online messaging, which showed in their audience reach. The Leave website had almost 400,000 more visits than the Remain site in the month before the referendum, but use of social media platforms was where the Leave group's awareness strategy was most convincing. Marciano (2016) showed that *Facebook* was the most important traffic source to websites, with 48.6% of traffic coming from *Facebook* and 15.6% from *Twitter*. However, Polonski (2016) suggested *Instagram* was the most useful for drawing online traffic to campaign messages. Campaigners on both sides posted images and memes on *Instagram* to encourage follows, likes and shares. Polonski (2016) showed that Brexit-supporters were more effective in their use of *Instagram* for activating and mobilising people across the country by using social media platforms. The most frequently used *Twitter* hashtags all expressed Leave sentiment:#brexit, #beleave and #voteleave.

One example of the way campaigners used social media more effectively than traditional news media was the use of *Facebook* by the far-right political party, *Britain First*. Much maligned within traditional news media, *Britain First* nonetheless had one of the most liked *Facebook* pages of all the political parties in the UK. Coming to public attention through a series of media stunts, the group's social media presence grew rapidly with almost 2 million likes, despite disdain within mainstream reportage. While the party's growth on social media gave organisers the ability to claim that a grassroots movement was occurring in the United Kingdom, it was estimated that less than a third of *Britain First*'s *Facebook* followers were actually genuine followers (Withnall 2015). Instead, social media users were being lured, sometimes unknowingly, to the page through the use of content such as colourful memes, quotes by popular figures, and statements on popular issues, invoking people to like multiple posts and draw indirect attention to *Britain First*. As Collins (2016) describes, 'Its colourful memes had a habit of popping up all over the place—against dog fighting, against child molestation, loving British soldiers, enthralling people to click "like" if they were wearing a poppy this year, and so on. The main problem was, few people actually knew what this group was or who was behind it'.

This type of 'click bait' is produced and disseminated cheaply and quickly, and the number of likes artificially manipulates *Facebook*'s prioritisation and filtering algorithms. *Facebook* has been using an algorithmic feed since very early in its existence, suggesting that the goal of its news feed was to 'show all the posts people want to see in the order they want to read them' (Backstrom 2013). Bucher (2012, p. 1) argues that platforms like *Facebook* treat a user's attention as a sociotechnical construct that emerges out of the organisation's governmental power over algorithmic decision-making. For example, *Facebook*'s algorithmic feed will prioritise what a user sees at the top of their news feed according to how often they interacted with a friend, page or public figure, the number of likes, shares and comments a post receives from you or others, and whether you have interacted with a post in the past. The news feed will also allow posts you did not see to 'reappear' at the top of the news feed if others have interacted with them (Backstrom 2013), though this is more heavily 'throttled' for individual *Facebook* pages. Social media like *Facebook* thus operates to implement an 'attention economy' aimed at influencing or structuring modes of engagement within the platform (Bucher 2012, p. 1).

These forms of directing attention and prioritisation differ slightly from the more traditional goals of a news organisation, which prioritises news events through a subjective decision-making process, based on professional, social and cultural norms, about what is most in the public interest that particular day. This prioritisation of audience engagement with content suggests that it is not the content itself, nor the user who posts it, that has the most bearing on what is prioritised in a user's news feed. Thus, *Britain First*'s use of clickable content meant user interaction would prioritise the group on other news feeds. It also meant that journalists and news organisations were competing with more content to ensure prioritisation in users' news feeds. In comparison, *Britain First*'s branded *Facebook* posts actually generated considerably fewer likes than posts by other parties, despite the campaigners being the most frequent posters of content (Goodway 2014). Furthermore, *Britain First* also seemed to struggle to maintain its following offline. Despite the large following on social media and the group's chairman claiming it had 6000 official members, support at rallies could often barely muster more than 100 people (Collins 2015).

Despite the lack of physical support, Leave campaigns like those supported by *Britain First* were effective because campaigners worked to 'reverse engineer' social media content to the desired outcome of increased votes (Tambini 2016). Rather than creating content that argued for the Leave vote, campaign messages were tested both online and in traditional media simply for their ability to gain attention. This proved successful, even if these messages were shown to be untrue in the traditional news media. Repeating the claims, in spite of the fact that they were not true, guaranteed discussion and, thus, more attention to the campaign message. The scepticism of the news media was thus irrelevant because the ultimate goal of the campaigners was merely attention and discussion of shared content, rather than the authenticity and credibility usually bestowed by traditional reportage on a political topic. After the campaigns had ended, groups such as *Britain First* dived in popularity. Furthermore, it was not campaign or media sites that got the most traffic after the referendum vote was known. Marciano (2016) found that UK online users flocked to the immigration pages of government websites globally, as well as currency exchange sites. For example, UK online user visits to Canada's immigration and citizenship site jumped 12% from 27,500 visits before the vote to 61,400 visits the day after (Marciano 2016). *GoogleTrends* (2016) reported that the second most popular question asked after Brexit by UK online users was: 'What is the EU?' This suggests that algorithmic manipulation of the prioritisation of news can be detrimental to public dialogue. Just as market-based strategy concerning news content in the newsroom was shown to act as a perverse incentive to journalists (see Chap. 4), it is also problematic for news organisations attempting to compete with other sources of news. While quantifying and creating rules that prioritise engagement with news does have benefits, including releasing journalists from time-limiting minutiae of reportage to concentrate on the more human, storytelling elements of reportage, the manipulation of this engagement for more political or strategic outcomes can diminish the social interests of public dialogue.

Conclusion

While Brexit showed that journalists now use data as an everyday method of reporting and analysing news events, political stakeholders adopted strategies that ensured prioritisation of their own content in the now all-important social media news feeds. While traditional journalism would generally provide credibility and authenticity to a political stakeholder's message through their reportage, the strategic use of prioritisation and filtering algorithms instead allowed their message to bypass media reportage in both popularity and distribution. This chapter has shown that the transition from the use of CAR to big data and algorithmic journalism has meant that the journalist has shifted from a central player in news production to a collaborator in a distributed and increasingly complex media environment. What has become apparent is that as data got bigger and more complex, the number of different actions needed to harness its potential in journalism properly has meant there are more stakeholders in the journalistic product. Programmers, web designers, data scientists and social media managers have also become implicated in the news cycle of research, production and distribution. Furthermore, the development of 'big' data in journalism from an individual tool of reportage to a large-scale, collaborative automation of reporting processes changes not just the production of news, but the role of the journalist within it.

This book now moves to the last consideration in the interconnected influences on the journalistic use of social media: journalism as an institution. In the preceding chapters, I have discussed the ways in which the production, reception and management of journalism have been influenced by (and have influenced) the technical, social and political characteristics of social media platforms. The concluding chapters of this book discuss those changes in the light of the ideological framework of journalism—the boundaries that have traditionally characterised the norms and behaviours that have placed journalism as the central gatekeeper in social life. These concluding chapters 'look forward' from the tradition of social authority of journalists to a new age of social journalism: an age of alternative truths and news distribution by like. What are the characteristics of journalism in an age of social media production and distribution of news, and what will the role of the news organisation and the journalist be within it?

References

Anderson, C. (2006). *The long tail: How the future of business is selling less of more*. New York, NY: Hyperion.

Anderson, C. W. (2013). Towards a sociology of computational and algorithmic journalism. *New Media and Society, 15,* 1005–1021.

Backstrom, L. (2013, August 7). News feed FYI: A window into news feed. *Facebook Business*. Retrieved from https://www.facebook.com/business/news/News-Feed-FYI-A-Window-Into-News-Feed.

Bringing Big Data to the Enterprise. (2017). IBM. Retrieved from https://www-01.ibm.com/software/data/bigdata/what-is-big-data.html.

Bucher, T. (2012). A technicity of attention: How software 'makes sense'. *Culture Machine, 13.* Retrieved from http://culturemachine.net/index.php/cm/article/viewDownloadInterstitial/470/489.

Burgess, M. (2016, April 4). How the 11.5 million Panama Papers were analysed. *Wired Offshore*. Retrieved from www.wired.co.uk/article/panama-papers-data-leak-how-analysed-amount.

Carbon Emissions: past, present and future-interactive. (2014, December 1). The Guardian. Retrieved from https://www.theguardian.com/environment/ng-interactive/2014/dec/01/carbon-emissions-past-present-and-future-interactive.

Carlson, M. (2015). The robotic reporter: Automated journalism and the redefinition of labour, compositional forms, and journalistic authority. *Digital Journalism, 3,* 416–431.

Chen, M., Shiwen, M., & Liu, Y. (2014). Big Data: A survey. *Mobile Networks and Applications, 19,* 171–209.

Cheney-Lippold, J. (2011). A new algorithmic identity: Soft biopolitics and the modulation of control. *Theory, Culture & Society, 28*(6), 164–181.

Coddington, M. (2015). Clarifying journalism's quantitative turn. A typology for evaluating data journalism, computational journalism, and computer-assisted reporting. *Digital Journalism, 3*(3), 331–338.

Collins, M. (2016, February 26). The truth about Britain First—The one-man band with a knack for Facebook. *The Guardian.* Retrieved from https://www.theguardian.com/commentisfree/2015/feb/25/truth-britain-first-facebook-far-right-bnp.

Deakon, D., Wring, D., Harmer, E., Stanyer, J., & Downey, J. (2016, June 16). Hard evidence: Analysis shows extent of press bias for Brexit. *The Conversation.* Retrieved from https://theconversation.com/hard-evidence-analysis-shows-extent-of-press-bias-towards-brexit-61106.

Diakopoulos, N. (2015). Algorithmic accountability: Journalistic investigation of computational power structures. *Digital Journalism, 3*(3), 398–415.

Dorr, K. N. (2016). Mapping the field of algorithmic journalism. *Digital Journalism, 4*(6), 700–722.

EU Referendum: The Results in Maps and Charts. (2016, June 24). BBC. Retrieved from http://www.bbc.com/news/uk-politics-36616028#orb-footer.

Feinberg, A. (2017, March 31). This is almost certainly FBI Director James Comey's Twitter account. *Gizmodo.* https://www.gizmodo.com.au/2017/03/this-is-almost-certainly-fbi-director-james-comeys-twitter-account/.

Gillespie, T. (2010). The politics of 'platforms'. *New Media & Society, 12*(3), 347–364.

Gillespie, T. (2014). The relevance of algorithms. In T. Gillespie, P. Boczkowski, & K. A. Foot (Eds.), *Media technologies: Essays on communication, materiality, and society.* Cambridge, MA: MIT Press. Retrieved from http://citeseerx.ist.psu.edu/viewdoc/download?doi=10.1.1.692.3942&rep=rep1&type=pdf.

Goodway, F. (2014, October 28). This is how Britain First plans to infiltarte your Facebook feed. Mirror. Retrieved from http://www.mirror.co.uk/news/ampp3d/how-britain-first-plans-infiltrate-4518320.

GoogleTrends. (2016, June 24). Top questions on the European Union. *Twitter.* Retrieved from https://twitter.com/GoogleTrends/status/746303118820937728.

Greenberg, A. (2016, April 4). How reporters pulled off the Panama Papers, the biggest leak in whistleblower history. *Wired.* Retrieved from www.wired.co.uk/article/.

Harding, L. (2016, April 5). What are the Panama Papers? A guide to history's biggest data leak. *The Guardian*. Retrieved from https://www.theguardian.com/news/2016/apr/03/what-you-need-to-know-about-the-panama-papers.

Henley, J. (2016, April 6). Iceland PM steps aside after protests over Panama Papers revelations. *The Guardian*. Retrieved from https://www.theguardian.com/world/2016/apr/05/iceland-prime-minister-resigns-over-panama-papers-revelations.

Hermida, A. (2014). *Tell everyone: Why we share and why it matters*. Toronto: Doubleday Canada.

Interview with Steve Suo. (2005, July 7). Frontline. Retrieved from http://www.pbs.org/wgbh/pages/frontline/meth/interviews/suo.html.

Jack, A. (2016a, January 2). 2016: Predictions and planning. *Financial Times*. Retrieved from https://www.ft.com/content/c699fbcc-b0a3-11e5-b955-1a1d298b6250.

Jack, I. (2016b, June 25). In this Brexit, the poor turned on an elite that ignored them. *The Guardian*. Retrieved from https://www.theguardian.com/commentisfree/2016/jun/25/brexit-vote-poor-elite.

Kanter, J. (2017, March 2). Leave.EU used 'creepy' Facebook profiling technology to win Brexit campaign—And now the government is investigating. *Business Insider*. Retrieved from https://www.businessinsider.com/leave-eu-brexit-creepy-facebook-cambridge-analytica-2017-2#tbyK8VM2S3FPXFGa.99.

Lewis, S. (2015). Journalism in an era of big data: Cases, concepts and critiques. *Digital Journalism, 3*(3), 321–330.

Lewis, S., & Usher, N. (2013). Open source and journalism: Toward new frameworks for imagining news innovation. *Media, Culture and Society, 35*(5), 602–619.

Lewis, S., & Westlund, O. (2014). Big data and journalism: Epistemology, expertise, economics and ethics. *Digital Journalism, 3*(3), 447–466.

Marciano, J. (2016, June 28). Who were the big online winners from Brexit? *Similar Web*. Retrieved from: https://www.similarweb.com/blog/brexit-traffic.

Meyer, P. (1979). *Precision journalism: A reporter's introduction to social science methods*. Bloomington: Indiana University Press.

Meyer, P. (2011, December 10). Riot theory is relative. *The Guardian*. Retrieved from https://www.theguardian.com/commentisfree/2011/dec/09/riot-theory-relative-detroit-england.

Miller, C. C. (2015, July 9). When algorithms discriminate. *The New York Times*. Retrieved from https://www.nytimes.com/2015/07/10/upshot/when-algorithms-discriminate.html.

Napoli, P. M. (2014). Automated media: An institutional theory perspective on algorithmic media production and consumption. *Communication Theory, 24*(3), 340–360.

Parasie, S., & Dagiral, E. (2013). Data-driven journalism and the public good: "Computer-assisted-reporters" and "programmer-journalists" in Chicago. *New Media & Society, 15*(6), 853–871.

Perraudin, F. (2016, December 9). Northern England's Brexit voters need to be heard, says thinktank. *The Guardian*. Retrieved from https://www.theguardian.com/politics/2016/dec/09/northern-englands-brexit-voters-need-to-be-heard-says-thinktank

Polonski, V. W. (2016, June 9). #Nofilter debate: Brexit campaigners dominate on Instagram. *The Conversation*. Retrieved from https://theconversation.com/nofilter-debate-brexit-campaigners-dominate-on-instagram-59933.

Sweney, M. (2016, June 29). Brexit breaks news records as Facebook helps drive leave campaign. *The Guardian*. Retrieved from https://www.theguardian.com/technology/2016/jun/29/brexit-breaks-news-records-as-facebook-proves-crucial-to-leave-victory.

Tambini, D. (2016, November 18). In the new robopolitics, social media has left newspapers for dead. *The Guardian*. Retrieved from https://www.theguardian.com/commentisfree/2016/nov/18/robopolitics-social-media-traditional-media-dead-brexit-trump.

Tandoc, E. C., & Thomas, R. J. (2015). The ethics of web analytics: Implications of using audience metrics in news construction. *Digital Journalism, 3*(2), 243–258.

Ten Predictions for 2016. (2016, January 1). *Al Jazeera English*. Retrieved from http://www.aljazeera.com/blogs/europe/2016/01/ten-predictions-2016-160101181341413.html.

The Hard-Headed Case for Britain to Stay in the EU. (2016, January 2). *Financial Times*. Retrieved from https://www.ft.com/content/ea8a0a6c-a415-11e5-873f-68411a84f346.

Withnall, A. (2015, November 10). Britain First far-right group claims to be 'first political party' to reach 1 million likes on Facebook. *The Independent*. Retrieved from http://www.independent.co.uk/news/uk/politics/britain-first-far-right-group-claims-to-be-first-political-party-to-reach-1-million-likes-on-a6728991.html.

CHAPTER 6

Shifting Values, New Norms: Social Media and the Changing Profession of Journalism

Natarsha Belling is a high-profile Australian journalist, instantly recognisable to television viewers as the presenter of a nightly television news programme for broadcaster *Network Ten*. Belling also participates in some other public roles, including serving on the Women's Advisory Board for the *National Breast and Ovarian Cancer Centre* and contributing to charity events, and is a budding social media influencer. While she has a relatively modest social media following of around 10,000 on each of her *Instagram* and *Twitter* accounts, her posts do not simply promote her news organisation or her professional work as a journalist. Amongst the more professionally oriented posts are others promoting a brand of footwear, a skin care range, and an Australian clothing designer. While many news organisations see this kind of promotion as unethical journalistic practice and create policies banning commercial promotion and acceptance of gifts, journalistic use of personal social media accounts for commercial promotion, can muddy this characterisation of their professional identity.

Behind the news stories of the day, there has always been the professional identity of the journalist. This is embodied not so much by journalists themselves, but by their adherence to particular professional norms of practice. Often journalistic practices are represented as part of the inherent personality or character of journalists, recognisable in film and literary representations of the tenacious, larrikin 'hack' determined to uncover a political scandal. While this is a generalisation of a journalist's role, these personal characteristics are often

D. Bossio, *Journalism and Social Media*,
DOI 10.1007/978-3-319-65472-0_6

highlighted as justification for a journalist's extraordinary professional authority to choose the events, people and discourses that shape representation of news and culture. This authority has been maintained by suggesting that journalism is a specialised profession, with claims to an exclusive role and status in society, based on a particular occupational ideology and associated professional characteristics (Deuze 2005, p. 442).

In the last chapters of this book, I investigate the institutional knowledge that frames journalism and how this is changing in social media environments. So far, I have discussed individual journalistic practice in Chaps. 2 and 3, and explored how online news creation and distribution models shift journalists away from 'one-way' communication models, and towards practices that are collaborative and engaged across social media platforms. The culture that has emerged around the affordances of social media technologies has prioritised openness, sharing, and the subjectivity of individualised interests—all of which negate the need for professional control over content creation (Lewis 2012, p. 837). Chapters 4 and 5 extended this analysis by illustrating how these changes in individual practice are influenced by the organisational structures journalists work within. Practices that conform to social media policies, as well as new relationships in the newsroom, were seen to create both opportunities and tensions in utilising social media for journalism. What many of these changes amount to, however, is a fundamental shift in the way professional journalism is understood and, subsequently, a steady erosion of the professional authority traditionally maintained by journalists.

While many of these changes have been widely discussed in the media and in academic research (see Livingstone and Asmolov 2010; Hermida 2012; Singer 2012; Domingo et al. 2008; Heinonen 2011; Heinrich 2011 for examples), this discussion has not always considered how the transition to online and social media has affected the construction and negotiation of professional identity in journalism (Lewis 2012; Molyneux and Holton 2015; Bossio and Sacco 2016). This chapter focusses on the ways journalists represent professional identity on popular social media platforms such as *Twitter*, *Facebook* and *Instagram*, using case studies drawn from different journalists' social media profiles. In doing so, this chapter illustrates how journalists are balancing individual, organisational and professional norms while transitioning journalistic professional activity into social media environments. The ways journalists present their personal and professional identities on social media seem to correspond with some of the complex professional and organisational influences they are attempting to balance. While some journalists are attempting to separate their online life from their professional work, others are constructing hybrid professional identities that include aspects of both their professional and personal lives. On the one hand, some journalists do seek to 'normalise' traditional norms of journalistic professional identity, such as objectivity and neutrality, in online spaces. On the other hand, many journalists are also actively seeking ways to utilise a more personal or 'authentic' tone engendered by social media cultures of audience participation. In between these needs are the editorial, organisational and institutional pressures that journalists negotiate to have a presence online.

Journalism as a Profession and Discourses of Professionalisation

To understand the ways journalists present their professional identity on social media, we must first consider the many complex debates that have occurred about how a journalistic professional identity can be constituted. For over 100 years, scholars and journalists have debated whether the occupation should be considered a profession, a trade or a craft. A good example of the complexity of these debates is Joseph Pulitzer's work to 'legitimise' journalism through the creation of the first academic journalism school at Columbia University in the United States. While there is no doubt that Pulitzer's contribution to modern, liberal journalism was immense, his editorial style did not always adhere to the ethical norms of modern professional journalism. At the time of his retirement, Pulitzer's reputation, as well as broader respect for journalism, had suffered due to overuse of sensationalist news content in daily newspaper reportage (Juergens 2015). These tabloid news practices were particularly evident in the often-fierce competition for readership with fellow news baron, William Hearst, a competition Pulitzer was said to regret later for its impact on the quality of his newspaper's journalism (Seitz 1927). However, an industry-wide push for better workplace standards, work on standardising ethical codes of practice and a better reputation for the industry itself meant that proprietors including Pulitzer, as well as journalists and other institutional authorities, saw the benefit of professionalisation. Pulitzer's plan was to legitimise journalism as a profession by taking away the trade-style apprenticeship model of journalism training and moving the skill set into the tertiary sector. In a model still utilised by some journalism schools, tertiary journalism education would teach 'the mission, duty and opportunity of the press as a moral teacher' (cited in Boylan 2003, p. 5). Thus, Pulitzer's plan for the professionalisation of journalism meant the articulation of a social identity for the journalist based on the articulation of their role in good governance. Journalism education could thus be seen as the acquisition of a 'democratic art', the quality of which would determine the benefits of democratic social life (Seitz 1927, p. 467). This marked the beginning of the articulation of the professionalised fourth estate role that journalists now espouse to legitimate their voice in political, social and cultural life.

The organisational development of journalism within newspapers came with an increasing social and political status that was subsequently acknowledged through an elite skill set within the academy. In Chap. 2, this skill set was seen to have been articulated through particular norms of behaviour, including practices of objectivity, verification and autonomy. While these norms of behaviour have been represented as now-reified professional practices, in reality the 'professionalisation' of journalism has not been so smooth. Within professional associations for journalism across the USA, Europe and Australia, the question of whether journalism has a common 'core of knowledge' continues to plague journalism practice. Traditionally, professionalisation closes off members of a profession from 'amateurs' through specialist skill or norms of practice. Journalism, however, does not have all the attributes that enable it to be called a 'profession'. A profession has been traditionally defined by its dependence upon specialised educational training, an association or code that regulates the conduct of members of the profession and a strong division between the knowledge and skills of those within the profession and those demarcated as 'amateur'—as Durkheim (2013) suggested, a kind of moral community based on occupational membership. This definition was problematised by early work in the sociology of the professions, where academics began to introduce new conceptions of professions, such as the social organisation of labour markets (Brint 1993). Barber (1963, p. 671) suggested instead that a sociological definition of the professions should only be defined by the specifics of professional behaviour—concepts such as 'style of life, corporate solidarity, socialisation structures and processes which apply to all other groups as well as professional ones'. Eventually, four aspects of a profession were identified as objects of study, including the division of labour, occupational communities, the social activity of work itself, and occupational rewards (Rothman 1998). More recently, focus has shifted to understanding the professionalisation process through which an occupational community establishes norms of conduct, organisational qualifications and distinction from 'outsiders'.

As the academic definition of professions moved away from a 'checklist of "traits"' (Aldridge and Evetts 2003, p. 548), understanding of professional journalism has focussed much more on occupational ideologies that ascribe professional behaviour to a larger institutional understanding of the occupation. Indeed, contemporary journalists have been much more likely to base their understanding of professional journalism on a discourse that sets journalistic behaviours and practices apart from other forms of knowledge, rather than a traditional set of legal or ethical requirements (Aldridge and Evetts 2003). This discourse of professionalism presents a justification for journalists having a powerful role in the governance of society through a claim to represent or act on behalf of the 'public'. Deuze (2005) has suggested this professional ideology fits a set of particular characteristics of professional journalism: service to the public, autonomy, objectivity, ethical practice and immediacy. It is only those who claim a professional and elite status through their expertise over these journalistic practices who can also claim social, cultural or political authority to speak about—and for—the governance of societies. The rights and responsibilities claimed by the 'professional' also establish their privilege over those who might do the same activities 'outside' professional status and self-identity. Thus, discourses of professionalism (rather than the conception of journalism as a profession) have been an important part of forming a journalist's professional self-identity (Zelizer 2004). As Lewis (2012, p. 845) suggests, journalists have gained much of their sense of social authority through their control of how information is represented in reportage, as well as their assumption of their sole claim to this role.

The Representation of Professional Identity in Journalism

Established discourses of professionalism affect the ways in which journalists present themselves to the public; the professional norms and values that indicate professional practice are discursively constructed and 'performed' to suggest a particular character that only a 'professional' journalist can possess. In the past, this performance of professional identity was generally only semi-public; a journalist's byline, voice on the radio or face presented on the evening television news came with an assumption of their professional and ethical values. But use of social media has made both professional identity and behaviour much more visible and accessible to interested audiences. While social media environments disrupt the centrality of the journalist in the news production and dissemination process, the performance of more traditional forms of professional self-identity has endured.

Professional identity has been defined as the understanding of self in a professional context—who you are and how you act as an individual and in groups within your particular organisation, institution or profession (Fredriksson and Bendt 2014). Professional identity is a social construct: the 'product of norms, practices and status tied to (1) a professional ideology, (2) organisational belonging, and (3) the individual's social position' (Wiik 2010). Each component affects the way a professional might present themselves and how they might conform to certain professional behaviours and values. Conforming to a particular performance of a socially correct professional behaviour also gives a person access to status and authority in society and enables others to acknowledge and trust in their behaviours as 'professional'.

The performance of particular forms of identity cuts across both professional and personal lives. Erving Goffman is perhaps best known for his focus on an individual's performance of self to others. Goffman (1959, p. 5) suggested that the self was a social product, using the analogy of the stage to illustrate the ways we present ourselves to others in different contexts. Social behaviours were divided into the 'front stage', where the self is visible and a person deliberately gives information about oneself, and the 'back stage', where the self is hidden from view and any information one 'gives off' is inadvertent (Goffman 1959, p. 20). This information allows comfortable social interactions because 'information about the individual helps to define the situation, enabling others to know in advance what he will expect of them and what they may expect of him' (Goffman 1959, p. 21). This suggests that a person's performance of identity defines the norms of behaviour in a given social situation. Goffman (1963) argued that people had a multiplicity of 'selves' and, accordingly, behaviours; in later work, he extended this by emphasising the different selves that play into the social roles required of a particular context. In these social roles, people can stay 'in role' and behave appropriately or 'break role' and behave inappropriately (Goffman 1963).

Though Goffman suggested that his theorisation of the presentation of self referred only to face-to-face interactions, there are connections to be made with the performance of identity in online environments. Social media platforms, for example, enable the representation of multiple versions of identity through interactions with others, and differ according to whom the individual interacts with and their social context. Early Internet scholars recognised the potential for a multiplicity of identity constructions in online spaces (Turkle 1995; boyd 2006) and their research highlighted the 'identity play' of individuals engaged in online chat, gaming, dating and blogging. While this formative research illustrated instances in which online spaces allowed people to present fluid identities (Davis 2011, p. 636), further research showed that online identities were not necessarily disconnected from offline contexts, but had connections to the lives people led 'offline' (Baym, 1998). More contemporary media research has shown that while many people may choose to alter, shape or experiment with their identities in online environments, anxieties and tensions arise when negotiating the various professional and personal contexts in which communication might take place. Indeed, the requirement to present a verifiable, singular identity as a professional, for example, may make it impossible to differ self-presentation strategies, creating tensions as diverse groups of people access profiles for different reasons (boyd 2008). For journalists attempting to present a uniform professional identity online, there are also many competing priorities, demands and contexts that complicate the representation of professional identity.

Where much of Goffman's work on the representation of identity suggested behaviour representing identity as having a 'front stage' and 'back stage', the context for representation of identity often collapses on social media platforms (Marwick and boyd 2011). Social media content instead prioritises authentic personal expression and, thus, social media profiles often reveal more personal detail than would occur in an offline professional context. Furthermore, the types of audiences a journalist might encounter on social media present issues concerning how to navigate professional and personal identity. There are two types of audience on social media with which journalists might negotiate interactions: firstly, the audience simply interested in the journalist and their professional identity. This type of audience wants to engage with the journalist and their life as a professional media worker. The second type of audience is interested in the journalist's professional product: the news. This second audience is engaging the journalist as a conduit for news, and the journalist might also engage with this audience for professional purposes, such as finding a source or a trending news item. To balance institutional ideologies and organisational pressures, as well as to maintain a sense of online 'authenticity' with multiple audience types creates what Marwick and boyd (2011, p. 126) describe as 'context collapse'—the sheer diversity of the audience complicates how a public persona or identity can be managed. For example, representation of identity on a platform like *Twitter* does not typically present many issues for a journalist presenting a professional identity because of the professional culture and content that has flourished on this platform. However, a platform like *Instagram*, where the boundaries between personal and professional representation are still not clear, could raise concerns about identity representation. A journalist wanting to present themselves only as a professional on a site like *Instagram* may be conflicted, not only by the nature of the interaction with the audience, but with the conception of the *Instagram* culture and audience itself (Marwick and boyd 2011, p. 115).

Professional Identity in the Online Age—the Journalist

If being 'personal' is crucial for journalists wanting to build a professional 'brand', yet 'authenticity' is key to the believability of this brand (Sanderson 2008), journalists must negotiate multiple, overlapping audiences by strategically concealing information, targeting tweets at different audiences and attempting to portray both an authentic and interesting personality (Marwick and boyd 2011, p. 122). For a journalist, this also means balancing editorial, organisational and institutional demands on how and what a professional journalist should present online. Journalists deal with this complexity in different ways. Some journalists take this as an opportunity to present a hybrid media identity, presenting aspects of their professional and personal lives online as an extension of their professional identity. Others deal with the complexity of their audience on social media platforms by falling back on traditional notions of professional journalistic practice to maintain a particular image of themselves and their practice online. These journalists use social media predominantly to extend their already established media personas, simply promoting and distributing their stories. Much scholarship on journalistic professional practice online has suggested that journalists often attempt to 'normalise' professional occupational ideologies within new media practices (Lasorsa et al. 2012; Singer 2005). However, Holton and Molyneux (2015) suggest this normalisation process either applies journalists' existing patterns and routines to new media formats, or creates new professional norms that account for the affordances of these platforms. Thus, most journalists are performing their traditional occupational ideologies while also developing methods of engaging with newer contexts for news creation by negotiating use of social media platforms.

Creating a professional divide between personal and professional interactions on social media has sometimes had material effects, such as the creation of different accounts on one platform, or enhanced security settings. Journalists who separate their personal and professional identities on social media also state clearly when they act as professional journalists and represent their media organisation, and when they post as individuals and represent themselves. What this separation indicates is that journalists transitioning from traditional to new modes of communication are negotiating a number of different (and often new) influences on their practice. For journalists who may be negotiating how much of their personal identity should interact with their professional persona on social media platforms, adherence to more traditional professional norms of objectivity, neutrality and civic-mindedness might also be a way to protect their professional credibility and avoid any negative consequences with their media organisation.

An example of the way some journalists have separated personal and professional representations of identity on social media can be seen in the presentation of social media accounts by Australian television journalist, Alexis Daish. Daish is an early career crime reporter at *Nine News Melbourne*, a prime-time television news programme for *Channel Nine*, a commercial network in Australia. While many of her colleagues at *Nine News* present solely professional profiles on social media, Daish has separate personal and professional accounts on various platforms. She maintains a professional *Twitter* account, attributed to her workplace, but with the proviso that 'views are my own'. Daish does provide some personal information in her profile statement, suggesting hobbies like running and love for coffee. Daish's *Twitter* account contains content mainly from aspects of her reporting responsibility: crime stories and updates on arrests in Melbourne. The tone of the account is typically journalistic—breaking news, as well as topics for which Daish has reporting responsibility. Some content focussed on Daish herself is generally about her professional life, such as winning an award for journalism. Despite the public, professional *Twitter* account, Daish maintains private *Facebook* and *Instagram* accounts, accessible only via an approved request. The accounts are easily identifiable, with her name and an accompanying profile photo showing Daish. Her *Instagram* account description also indicates that she is a reporter for *Nine News*, and the accompanying image is a professional *Nine News* photo. However, the separation of private and public accounts suggests either some compliance with an organisational social media policy, or her personal concern that her professional identity should be kept separate from her personal views and life outside her work. This is indicative of the themes that emerge on her public social media platforms: firstly, promotion of the 'real' or 'more important' tasks of journalism, and secondly, of individual brand-driven content.

While use of social media has presented a number of different possibilities for engagement with sources and audiences, journalists such as Daish have sometimes drawn sharp distinctions between presenting professional and personal identities online. In the past, Daish's identity as a broadcast journalist would have been recognisable by voice or appearance, but would never have revealed any aspects of her personal character. On social media, however, Daish makes a choice about whether tweets about breaking news might sit side by side with an account of her hobbies, daily life and personal political preferences. Adding a personal identity to a name might be somewhat more difficult for a journalist, especially when traditional occupational ideologies still demand certain values like objectivity and neutrality. Nonetheless, despite journalists such as Daish attempting to normalise professional journalistic use of social media, this separation of professional and personal identity on social media is increasingly being contested. News organisations are now routinely asking journalists to incorporate social media interaction into their daily reporting routines, in the hope that these personal interactions will send more 'eyeballs' towards their organisational web presence. Journalists themselves are also increasingly using social media to interact with sources and users as a form of professional 'branding' tied not to their organisations, but to their own institutional identities. This has resulted in a number of different approaches to the presentation of professional identity online.

Professional Identity in the Online Age—Organisations

While an individual journalist's concept of their own professional identity might influence their representation on social media, larger organisational interests might also limit or expand individual professional representation and behaviour online. Evetts (2003) suggests that there is a difference between 'occupational professionalism', as the professional ideology that structures the way individual journalists characterise and value their professional practices, and the 'organisational professionalism' that allows organisations to emphasise compliance with professional standards. While both forms of professionalism seek to characterise professional behaviour, there are often divergent opinions about how those behaviours should be expressed in practice. These differences become apparent in the individual and organisational use of social media for journalism.

News organisations have sometimes focussed on social media as a commercial problem to be solved. Traditional news organisations and journalistic practices have continued to be an important source of what is perceived as news for audiences. In Chap. 4, the traditional business model of commercial and classified advertising was discussed as the traditional financial support for expensive journalistic practice, but as this business model has become disrupted by online and social media, news organisations have found it increasingly difficult to retain not just revenue, but audiences too. In this environment, social media has often been embraced as a promotional, rather than editorial, tool within news organisations. News organisations have increasingly implemented structural and managerial changes to encourage journalists to utilise social media as a way to promote and distribute their own work, and to encourage audiences to click through to the larger news organisation's web presence. For example, larger news organisations have encouraged new professional relationships in the newsroom between journalists and social media or community managers to encourage the use of social media to promote the news organisation and its branded content online (Bossio and Sacco 2016). Apart from the promotional use of social media, news organisations have also established social media guidelines, policies and training to maintain particular forms of professional behaviour online. These have ranged from strict policies concerning journalistic behaviour online to more pragmatic training sessions discussing 'best practice' on social media.

There are, nonetheless, tensions between the individual journalists' need for promotional and editorial use of social media and the larger news organisations' perspective on maintaining the credibility of the news brand. We see this tension when a journalist uses social media as a form of personal communication, but this clashes with the public, professional persona that frames their social media profile. For example, the Australian multicultural broadcaster *SBS* stirred controversy when its managing director, Michael Ebeid, and director of sport, Ken Shipp, said that comments made on social media by a popular television soccer journalist, Scott McIntyre, made his employment 'untenable' (Chalmers 2015). McIntyre had used *Twitter* to comment on an Australian public holiday, ANZAC day, which commemorates the anniversary of the first major military operation fought by both Australian and New Zealand during the First World War. While much of the commentary on ANZAC day typically focusses on the heroism of the ANZAC forces, McIntyre was more critical. He tweeted to his 30,000 followers: 'Wonder if the poorly-read, largely white, nationalist drinkers and gamblers pause today to consider the horror that all mankind suffered.' He followed this with another tweet: 'Remembering the summary execution, widespread rape and theft committed by these "brave" Anzacs in Egypt, Palestine and Japan.' He tweeted another three times about Australia's involvement in different military campaigns.

Unsurprisingly, the tweets garnered both support and condemnation, but drew much more public attention when Australia's communications minister (now prime minister of Australia), Malcolm Turnbull, disparaged the journalist. Replying on *Twitter*, Turnbull tweeted: 'Difficult to think of more offensive or inappropriate comments than those by @mcintinhos. Despicable remarks [sic] deserve to be condemned.' Turnbull also personally rang the managing director to register his dissatisfaction with the comments. By the next day, McIntyre had lost his job and *SBS* released a press statement damning his actions, saying that McIntyre had breached the *SBS* Code of Conduct and social media policy (in Whitebourn 2015). The incident triggered much debate about whether journalists should be able to voice their personal opinion on social media and how much jurisdiction news organisations should have over the individual social media profiles of their staff. Some journalists suggested that firing McIntyre impeded his personal right to free speech, but other commentators suggested that organisationally branded social media profiles must comply with the social media policies of the organisation. This debate was reflected in the legal 'stoush' that ensued. When McIntyre subsequently lodged a complaint with the Fair Work Commission of Australia, arguing that he had been unfairly dismissed because of his political views, *SBS* argued that his dismissal was due to his breach of the organisation's social media policy (Chalmers 2016). While the company settled before the case went to trial, the union that represents journalists in Australia, the *Media, Entertainment and Arts Alliance*, warned that vaguely worded social media policies had 'begun to infringe on the private lives of media professionals, dictating what they can and can't say in a private capacity, outside of their work' (in Chalmers 2015). This incident sits among many other examples across the world of journalists running afoul of their employers because a personal or subjective view published on social media did not match the organisation's professional standards or reputational interests. Some journalists have suggested that concern about organisational jurisdiction over their personal social media profiles has had a 'chilling' effect on what they publish on social media (Bossio and Sacco 2016) and thus they restrict information and opinion in their public posts. Other journalists are dismissive of social media policy, suggesting that 'common sense' or the values promoted by occupational professionalism should also frame their professional practice online (Steenson 2016).

The issues that emerge from organisational influence on journalistic representation of professional identity on social media are framed by two interconnected considerations; the first is implied by Evetts' (2003) distinction between the occupational and organisational understanding of professional behaviour and the second by the clash between the promotional and editorial use of social media by both journalists and news organisations. This creates tensions when there is a mismatch between the journalist's and the social media manager's professional expectations of social media use and management in the newsroom. This often stems from the inherent complexity of organisational needs for social media in the newsroom—balancing the editorial and training demands of those working in the newsroom with the brand promotion and reputational protection demanded by the executive levels of the organisation. Similarly, the expectations of journalists, particularly those used to working within a professional culture of individualism and autonomy, might clash with the collaborative and audience-focussed nature of the relationship with a social media manager.

Where some organisations have taken an 'editorial' approach to social media management within the newsroom, using community managers to support the sourcing and dissemination of news and providing industry-centred training on journalistic use of social media, many others have focussed on organisational branding. This has meant a mix of personal branding and promotion of the individual journalist, as well as organisationally focussed branding and reputational management of content posted on the social media platforms. A good example of this is the social media profiles of news 'personalities' for the major broadcast channels in Australia. Journalists working for *Nine News*, the news programme for the broadcast *Channel Nine,* have been required by their employer to change their social media handles to incorporate 'nine' after their name to increase the visibility of the news organisation's brand online. Many broadcasters from other stations have followed suit, effectively 'branding' their profile and content through their organisational affiliation.

In this context, some journalists choose to present only their professional identity on social media. Australian journalist and celebrity broadcaster Peter Hitchener's social media profile is a good example of a strictly professional and promotional use of social media. Hitchener has been the chief presenter of *Nine News*, a major metropolitan news service in Melbourne, Australia, for 16 years and has a large public profile. Apart from revealing his homosexuality in a newspaper interview in 2008, Hitchener's private life is largely absent from online and social media. His profile on the *Nine News* web page is a description of his career trajectory and highlights, though there is mention in the last paragraph that 'Hitchener lives in inner suburban Melbourne. He enjoys the occasional hit of tennis or round of golf and is a lifelong supporter of the Australian Rules St Kilda Football Club' (Meet the Team, n.d.). A professional website in his name is also dedicated to his charity work, as well as linking to other media work like his car review podcast.

Hitchener's public social media profiles include *Facebook*, *Instagram* and *Twitter*. Similarly to most *Nine News* journalists, all his social media handles end with the number nine, indicating his professional link to the channel. Almost all Hitchener's social media content comprises scenes or text related to his professional life as a presenter for a major metropolitan news channel. Hitchener's *Twitter* account contains three types of content: tweets about breaking news with a link to the *Nine News* website, forward promotion of news stories to appear on the evening bulletin or other media where he will appear and, finally, images of Melbourne. Hitchener's retweets are predominantly from *Nine News' Twitter* feed and, less commonly, forward promotion from other media organisations if they mention an appearance by Hitchener. Similarly, Hitchener's *Instagram* account is dominated by behind the scenes images of Hitchener's workday at the news broadcaster. There are images of him smiling with colleagues, at the presenter's desk or doing promotional or charity work. Other images are mainly photographs of iconic Melbourne scenes. While all the posts indicate Hitchener's 'authorial voice', none of the social media profiles indicates a life beyond Hitchener's work as a professional journalist. The profile is representative of work performance and professional identity and it appears, from surveying other *Nine News* journalists with large public profiles, that this use of social media is consistent across the media organisation.

This representation suggests that Hitchener may be adhering strictly to social media policy and the protections that it affords, but the content also suggests social media is being used as an extra promotional tool utilising Hitchener's organisational and professional identity. This type of 'branding' often manifests in journalists' social media profiles—on both an individual and organisational level. While branding practices on the individual level focus on the journalist's personal identity as a way to build trust and engagement with an audience, branding practices on the organisational level seek to promote the journalist's professional reputation 'off the back' of the reputation and credibility of the news organisation's brand. This can be problematic when the discourses of organisational professionalism that seek to make journalists comply with professional standards based on commercial and reputational concerns clash with the occupational ideologies that allow journalists to assert their relevance and authority.

Professional Identity in the Online Age—Institutions

Changes in a journalist's professional mission and routines have significant ramifications for the profession and, of course, for the professional identity of the journalist. The previous examples in this chapter have illustrated the ways in which normalising professional norms on social media or prioritising the promotional potential of news leads to particular representations of professional identity online. Some scholars have suggested that these normalising practices have meant that both journalists and newsrooms have found themselves out of step with contemporary media trends—and for good reason. Newsrooms were slow to embrace the changes wrought by online communications and journalists themselves were wary of the lack of verification and speed that online practices often embraced. Hermida (2012) argues that news organisations 'have largely transferred existing norms and practices to new media, rather than taking on the open and participatory ethos of Web 2.0 tools and services'. While this might have been the case initially, more recent journalism has illustrated a period of transition, where practitioners are slowly expanding their online skills. Some journalists are selectively expanding their existing everyday methods, using basic social media practices such as monitoring and disseminating links to news, but are still mostly relying on traditional professional norms and practices (Tandoc et al. 2013). However, if the disruptive potential of social media for journalistic practice illustrates one thing, it is that the discourses of professionalism that underpin them are continually changing and that journalists and other media practitioners are often at the forefront of responding to that change.

Holton (2016) has suggested that freelance journalists have been particularly innovative in utilising social media to construct and maintain audiences through representation of an 'authentic' professional identity. Holton (2016) found freelance journalists were not as restricted by organisational policies about behaviour on social media and thus coupled posts about news with informed opinion, details of their lives and direct engagement with audiences. It is ironically this engagement with audiences that increases a freelancer's work opportunities because media organisations value the networks and interactions that this representation of hybrid identity has facilitated on social media (Holton 2016). An increasing number of journalists can be seen to be incorporating much more 'hybrid' professional and personal characteristics in their social media practice. Journalists such as Kevin Anderson, *The Guardian's* first blogs editor, and Jess Hill, former Australian *ABC* investigative journalist, have described how using more 'personalised' forms of online engagement through social media has enabled their journalism. These more personalised forms of engagement with social media audiences included using a more personal discursive tone, engaging with individual social media users, using crowdsourcing methods to investigate news stories and being collaborative and transparent in the investigation and production of news stories (see Chap. 2). Many of these practices are still professional in nature, but adhere to cultures of 'authentic' expression on social media, where more personal interaction with audience members leads to more engaged forms of journalistic practice.

While Hedman and Djerf-Pierre (2013, p. 372) suggest that journalists' use of social media can be seen as part of an increasing audience orientation, it could also be seen as a component of the personal and corporate promotion of news organisations. Other journalists might present a hybrid version of these forms of engagement, depending on the complexity of negotiating personal and professional content on social media. If the 'contextlessness' of social media platforms and their ambient nature make it easier to intertwine personal and professional lives online, it may be that journalists also combine different priorities when communicating the news on social media. For example, Latika Bourke is an Australian journalist who uses a mix of personal and professional social media content to report for *Fairfax* from London on European and Australian politics. Bourke was a former social media reporter for *ABC* and was named the 2010 Walkley Young Australian Journalist of the year for her coverage of the Liberal leadership crisis that saw Tony Abbott topple Malcolm Turnbull. The Walkley Advisory Board agreed that Bourke's pioneering use of *Twitter* as the drama reached its climax in the party room added an important dimension to her reporting. Bourke gained over 100,000 followers on her *Twitter* account after the 2010 election; she also has an active *Instagram* account with almost 10,000 followers. On *Facebook*, Bourke has created a professional page, which currently has 13,000 likes. The content is largely professional and reports on daily events in Australian politics, though Bourke couples this with personal comment and some promotion of her book, *From India with Love*.

Bourke's *Twitter* account also contains predominantly journalistic content about federal politics, but is more irreverent in tone and often makes light of federal politics. This reflects the culture on the platform itself, which has been used as a tool for serious discussion and research, as well as audience engagement and personal branding (Hedman 2015, 2016). Bourke's *Instagram* account is much more personal, containing very few images from her life as a journalist. Instead the account portrays a representation of Bourke's seemingly glamorous lifestyle, such as images of her Porsche, her 'Paleo' diet and images of fashion purchases. In all, the *Instagram* account is a completely different representation of Bourke compared with her slightly more serious *Twitter* account. Bourke thus uses different social media platforms—and their associated cultures—to represent different aspects of her personal and professional identities. Moreover, she uses different social media platforms to present and frame different aspects of her professional ideology—posting promotional content and breaking news stories alternately. This seemingly 'hybrid' characterisation of her professional and personal lives presented on social media shows Burke's negotiation of the boundaries of journalistic professionalism to suit both her own practice and her own occupational ideology. For some journalists, operating personal social media accounts means a separation from their professional lives. But for increasing numbers of journalists, using a personal profile is part of the active construction of a brand with a better 'market value' for their product—which is both the news and themselves as 'news and opinion hubs' (Brems et al. 2017).

Conclusion

While new forms of engagement with sources and audiences on social media are now important journalistic tools, journalists are still transitioning into the creation of an online presence that not only adheres to their self-conception as a professional journalist, but also reveals enough of their character to be seen as an 'authentic' member of social media publics. Furthermore, everyday journalistic practice is subject to the organisational strategies and policies that may shape or, in fact, dictate the way a journalist frames their professional identity online. To do this, we must go beyond the usual descriptions of a binary opposition between normative and aspirational journalistic practice online to illustrate the number of issues that impact on the way journalists seek to present themselves online. Understanding of personal identity, and reliance on a traditional ideology of professional practice, editorial and institutional pressures all impact on the ways in which journalists use social media, the way in which they engage with their audiences, and by extension the way in which audiences engage with them. The context through which journalists both present themselves and engage with audiences illuminates the complexities of the introduction of social media to professional practice, but also the ways these interactions are changing, often led by journalists transitioning their practice into more social media-enabled forms of communication.

In this chapter, we have explored the way professional journalism has been constituted and its presentation and negotiation on social media as a representation of professional and personal identity. In the next chapter, we extend this discussion to investigate the product of those professional ideologies and norms—news and information. Chapter 7 will consider the changes brought to news production and products by the use of social media as a mode of communication, and how the specific characteristics of social media platforms have changed the way news is produced, presented and disseminated. This chapter discusses the changes to what we think about as 'news' and how we access it, especially in an era of algorithmic manipulation and 'fake news'.

References

Aldridge, M., & Evetts, J. (2003). Rethinking the concept of professionalism: The case of journalism. *The British Journal of Sociology, 54*(4), 547–564.

Barber, B. (1963). Some problems in the sociology of the professions. *Daedalus, 92*(4), 669–688.

Baym, N. (1998). The emergence of online community. In S. Jones (Ed.), *Cybersociety 2.0: Revisiting Computer Mediated Communication and Community* (pp. 35–68). Thousand Oaks, CA: Sage.

Bossio, D., & Sacco, V. (2016). Don't tweet this! How journalists and media organisations negotiate tensions emerging from the implementation of social media policy in newsrooms. *Digital Journalism, 5*(2), 177–193.

boyd, d. (2006). Friends, friendsters and myspace top 8: Writing community into being on social network sites. *First Monday, 11*(2) Retrieved from http://firstmonday.org/article/view/1418/1336.

boyd, d. (2008). Taken out of context: American teen sociality in networked publics. PhD dissertation, University of California Berkeley.

Boylan, J. (2003). *Pulitzer's School: Columbia University's School of Journalism, 1903–2003.* USA: Columbia University Press.

Brems, C., Temmerman, M., Graham, T., & Broersma, M. (2017). Personal branding on Twitter: How employed and freelance journalists stage themselves on social media. *Digital Journalism, 5*(4), 443–459.

Brint, S. (1993). Eliot Freidson's contribution to the sociology of professions. *Work and Occupations, 20*(3), 259–278.

Chalmers, M. (2015, April 27). Media Union challenges fairness of social media policies after Scott McIntyre dismissal. *The New Matilda.* Retrieved from https://newmatilda.com/2015/04/27/media-union-challenges-fairness-social-media-policies-after-scott-mcintyre-dismissal/.

Chalmers, M. (2016, April 11). SBS deletes media statement after settling with Scott McIntyre over ANZAC Day tweets. *The New Matilda.* Retrieved from https://newmatilda.com/2016/04/11/sbs-deletes-media-statement-after-settling-with-scott-mcintyre-over-anzac-day-tweets/.

Davis, K. (2011). Tensions of identity in a networked era: Young people's perspectives on the risks and rewards of online self-expression. *New Media and Society, 14*(4), 634–651.

Deuze, M. (2005). What is journalism? Professional identity and ideology of journalists reconsidered. *Journalism, 6*(4), 442–464.

Domingo, D., Quandt, T., Heinonen, A., Paulussen, S., Singer, J. B., & Vujnovic, M. (2008). Participatory journalism practices in the media and beyond: An international comparative study of initiatives in online newspapers. *Journalism Practice, 2*(3), 326–342.

Durkheim, E. (2013). *Professional ethics and civic morals* (3rd ed.). London: Routledge.

Evetts, J. (2003). The sociological analysis of professionalism: Occupational change in the modern world. *International Sociology, 18*(2), 395–415. http://dx.doi.org/10.1177/0268580903018002005.

Fredriksson, M., & Bendt, J. (2014). The Dynamics of Professional Identity. *Journalism Practice, 8*(5), 585–595.

Goffman, E. (1959). *The presentation of self in everyday life*. London: Allen Lane The Penguin Press.

Goffman, E. (1963). *Stigma: Notes on the management of spoiled identity*. New York: Schuster & Schuster.

Hedman, U. (2015). J-Tweeters. *Digital Journalism, 3*, 279–297.

Hedman, U. (2016). When journalists tweet: Disclosure, participatory, and personal transparency. *Social Media + Society, 2*(1), http://dx.doi.org/2056305115624528.

Hedman, U., & Djerf-Pierre, M. (2013). The social journalist. *Digital Journalism, 1*(3), 368–385.

Heinonen, A. (2011). The journalist's relationship with users: New dimensions to conventional roles. In J. B. Singer, D. Domingo, A. Heinonen, A. Hermida, S. Paulussen, T. Quandt, Z. Reich, & M. Vujnovic (Eds.), *Participatory journalism: Guarding open gates at online newspapers* (pp. 34–55). West Sussex: Wiley.

Heinrich, A. (2011). *Network journalism: Journalistic practice in interactive spheres*. Hoboken, NY: Routledge.

Hermida, A. (2012). Social journalism: Exploring how social media is shaping journalism. In E. Siapera & A. Veglis (Eds.), *The handbook of global online journalism* (pp. 309–328). West Sussex: Wiley.

Holton, A. E. (2016). Intrapreneurial Informants. *Journalism Practice*. Retrieved from http://dx.doi.org/10.1080/17512786.2016.1166069.

Holton, A. E., & Molyneux, L. (2015). Identity lost? The personal impact of brand journalism. *Journalism*. http://dx.doi.org/10.1177/1464884915608816.

Juergens, G. (2015). *Joseph Pulitzer and the New York world*. Princeton: Princeton University Press.

Lasorsa, D. L., Lewis, S. C., & Holton, A. (2012). Normalizing twitter: Journalism practice in an emerging communication space. *Journalism Studies, 13*(1), 19–36.

Lewis, S. (2012). The tension between professional control and open participation. *Information, Communication & Society, 15*(6), 836–866.

Livingstone, S., & Asmolov, G. (2010). Networks and the future of foreign affairs reporting. *Journalism Studies, 11*(5), 745–760.

Marwick, A., & boyd, d. (2011). I Tweet Honestly, I Tweet Passionately: Twitter Users, Context Collapse, and the Imagined Audience. *New Media and Society, 13*(1), 114–133. doi: 10.1177/1461444810365313.

Meet the Team. (n.d). *Nine News*. Retrieved from http://www.9news.com.au/meet-the-team/melbourne/peter-hitchener.

Molyneux, L., & Holton, A. (2015). Branding (Health) journalism. *Digital Journalism, 3*(2), 225–242.

Rothman, R. (1998). *Working: Sociological perspectives*. Upper Saddle River, NJ: Prentice Hall.

Sanderson, J. (2008). The blog is serving its purpose: Self-presentation strategies on 38pitches.com. *Journal of Computer-Mediated Communication, 13*(4), 912–936.

Seitz, D. (1927). *Joseph Pulitzer, his life and letters*. USA: Garden City Publishing Co.

Singer, J. (2005). The political J-blogger: 'Normalising' a new media form to fit old norms and practices. *Journalism, 6*(2), 173–198.

Singer, J. (2012). The ethics of social journalism. *Australian Journalism Review, 34*(1), 3–16.

Steenson, S. (2016). The intimization of journalism. In T. Witschge, C. W. Anderson, D. Domingo, & A. Hermida (Eds.), (pp. 113–127). *The SAGE Handbook of Digital Journalism*. London: Sage.

Tandoc, E. C., Hellmueller, L., & Vos, T. P. (2013). Mind the gap: Between journalistic role conception and role enactment. *Journalism Practice, 7*(5), 539–554.

Turkle, S. (1995). *Life on the Screen: Identity in the Age of the Internet*. New York: Simon and Schuster.

Whitebourn, M. (2015, April 26). SBS presenter Scott McIntyre sacked over 'inappropriate' Anzac Day tweets. *Sydney Morning Herald*. Retrieved from http://www.smh.com.au/national/ww1/sbs-presenter-scott-mcintyre-sacked-over-inappropriate-anzac-day-tweets-20150426-1mtbx8.html.

Wiik, J. (2010). *Journalism in Transition. The Professional Identity of Swedish Journalists*. Institutionen for Journalistik, medier och kommunikation: Goteborgs Universitet.

Zelizer, B. (2004). *Taking journalism seriously: News and the academy*. Thousand Oaks, CA: Sage.

CHAPTER 7

News in Social Media Environments: Journalism in a 'Post-Truth' World

The accusations began to roll in almost immediately after Donald Trump declared his intent to run as the Republican nominee for president of the United States. Trump, according to much of the mainstream news media, is a purveyor of 'fake' news: unsubstantiated assertions distributed through social media that serve to divert critical attention away from his actual policies. On the other hand, Trump suggests that he is in fact the victim of fake news, often using his popular *Twitter* account to suggest that journalists emphasise unsubstantiated rumours and mockery to discredit him. The issue of whether news audiences are being fed 'fake news' by media and political stakeholders is more complicated than the simple accusations being thrown around in recent American politics. So far, this book has shown that social media distribution of news constantly disrupts the dominance of both traditional media and political stakeholders over the representation of 'truth'. Thus, these public tussles between politicians and journalists appear to be more about who has more institutional influence over public dialogue. Since the election of Donald Trump to the US presidency, journalists and audiences have continually had to negotiate what can be relied upon as news; indeed, the social media-enabled distribution of fake news suggests that perhaps truth is the last frontier of online news environments.

This chapter considers the changes brought by social media to understanding of journalism as a mode of distributing news and information. While the previous chapter focussed on the norms and ideologies that frame journalism as a profession, this chapter broadens discussion of the

D. Bossio, *Journalism and Social Media*,
DOI 10.1007/978-3-319-65472-0_7

characterisation of journalism to its product—news and its distribution. Traditionally, journalists and their news organisations have been at the centre of professional practices that decide what a 'true' representation of news might be, and how it should be delivered to an audience. However, this chapter argues that new modes of producing news and new business models for distributing news have resulted in the decentralisation of the journalist and news organisation from the communication of news. There are now more stakeholders in the selection and distribution of news and, thus, continual negotiation of representations of truth and the right to determine how it is distributed to audiences.

The chapter begins by outlining the historical and political context for the centrality of journalists and news organisations in the selection and distribution of 'true' news events. As online and social media continually disrupt these traditional modes of producing and distributing news, governance over 'truth' as central to communication is also being re-negotiated by new stakeholders in the news. This is evidenced by media coverage of Trump's use of false statements during his 2016 election campaign and his first days as president of the United States. These false statements, as well as their immediate distribution and amplification through social media, created dilemmas for journalists attempting to retain traditional norms of reportage. The ability for 'fake news' to gain traction on social media and the subsequent 'mainstreaming' of these falsehoods through news reportage meant that even if reporters were clarifying these falsehoods with truth, it was these falsehoods that actually became 'the news'. This suggests some of the challenges that social media production and distribution of news brings to institutional understanding of journalism. Greater opportunities to collaborate and represent diverse viewpoints in the news using the various affordances of social media are coupled with the tensions created by other social and political stakeholders with interests in influencing what this news should be.

Production and Distribution of News—An Historical and Political Context

Donald Trump's various interventions into the news cycle, with false accusations about everything from the legitimacy of Barack Obama's birth certificate to Hillary Clinton's health, show that truth is no longer the singular domain of journalists. It seems that Trump's ability to make these interventions into the news is empowered by the production and distribution affordances enabled by social media platforms—and how these have changed the institutional understanding of journalism's dominance over the news agenda. The traditional norms and ideologies that underpin professional journalism have been developed through the framework of print and broadcast production and distribution practices. Journalists' daily routines were once centred on individual practices of uncovering news and meeting print or broadcast deadlines for daily distribution of news. These practices were at the centre of the production cycle, with supporting and management roles given to news desk editors and their deputies. For example, in a traditional newspaper newsroom, operational roles are hierarchical, divided by production focus and time bound to printing (Pape and Featherstone 2005). A typical newsroom would be staffed by general and specialised news reporters, and managed by a host of specialised editors responsible for subjective decisions about which stories would lead the news and which journalists would cover them. Similarly, a news editor would be tasked with finding stories by aggregating news from national news agencies, checking the news diary for pre-planned events or commissioning 'fluff' pieces (Pape and Featherstone 2005, p. 3). Much of the rest of news production would occur outside the central news desk—subeditors sat separately from journalists and worked on designing pages, laying out stories, and adding headlines, bylines and captions, only contacting a journalist to check their copy for grammatical or legal issues. Similarly, while photographers routinely accompanied journalists on stories, they performed their news functions separately and had separate editors. Staff responsible for advertising sales were not even considered part of the daily production of news, and were often housed out of sight of the newsroom, despite the centrality of advertising to the financial sustainability of traditional news operations.

Much of the structure of the newsroom and the organisation of labour revolved around the production and distribution of the particular news product. For example, journalists generally filed stories for afternoon deadlines, based on the schedule for efficient printing and delivery of newspapers. Broadcast newsrooms worked according to similar organisational structures, but with many more staff dedicated to editing and production of audio and video content. The industrialised processes of printing and broadcasting therefore had an impact on the organisational structures and processes of producing journalism, which in turn was one of the factors affecting the constitution of journalism's professional practices. While the ideological framework that supports professional practice prioritises the need for a democratic public sphere to be kept informed, journalism is also influenced by the economic, organisational and structural processes (and pressures) that aid its production. Thus, as argued in Chap. 3, institutional understanding of the role of journalists and journalism cannot be separated from the business models, modes of production and distribution that underpin traditional news practices.

As newer technologies and their associated modes of production have been gradually introduced into the newsroom, they have also disrupted traditional understandings of journalism practice. For example, the introduction of 24-hour news broadcasting and online publishing brought new modes of presenting and focussing attention on important news events. Indeed, political scientists have referred to the 'CNN-effect' as the way sustained coverage of events from media outlets encourages more attention from audiences and can thus encourage political or social action on particular issues (Robinson 2005). This attention, however, also created issues for journalists forced to produce 'new information' continually about events they were covering, leading to a blurred line between information and entertainment in the production of news events. This was a particular critique of the unprecedented levels of media coverage of the 2003 war in Iraq, when some embedded journalists were accused of overdramatising or using false information about the Iraqi government and people, including staging news events for the cameras (Aday et al. 2005).

Similarly, the introduction of online publishing of news saw increased opportunities for new presentation styles, faster publication and broader distribution of news. Blogs and news website publication, coupled with cheaper media production tools, have enabled many more viewpoints and news production styles to flourish online. In previous chapters, I have discussed the opportunities that online news publication has provided for increased public dialogue and positive social change through collaborative reportage and wider audience reach. With those changes, however, has come the increasing pressure on legacy news organisations to sustain the production of journalism without traditional advertising revenues. Chapter 4 showed that this has meant large-scale redundancies and scaling back of resources for reportage, as well as increased time and labour pressures on journalists. Just as the ease of online publication has allowed more viewpoints to be accessible to audiences, there have accordingly been issues ensuring the veracity of information found online. The changes in these production and distribution methods have also affected the way the role of journalism has been constituted, with professional journalists now expected to have multimedia production skills, and to be collaborative and entrepreneurial in their professional conduct. Social media has brought another layer of complexity to the individual journalist's daily work, as well as organisational and institutional changes to the characterisation of this work.

News Production and Distribution Enabled by Social Media

While early iterations of social media platforms were focussed on individual expression and creating networks, newer formats have seen the increased opportunities to create and share original content. Thus, information flows on social media platforms are influenced by the unique forms of distribution that have developed over time (Burgess and Bruns 2012). News flows on social media have become prominent through individual sharing and the groups created through engagement with particular events, topics or trends. The characteristic ways that news flows through social media networks, using the features of specific platforms, has had particular influences on journalistic practice. For example, *Twitter*'s 'live tweeting' feature has become an important reporting practice, where both eyewitnesses and professional journalists have the ability to report events on the ground. This might involve one-off incidents such as the forcible removal of a passenger from a United Airlines flight in 2017, or emergency incidents such as the 2016 terror attacks in Nice, where eyewitnesses shared descriptions in text, as well as video, audio or photo footage of events as they occurred. Similarly, journalists and individual users respond to live tweeting of events through re-tweeting or using hashtags to engage in a conversation about news events. Burgess and Bruns (2012, p. 802) suggest these popular forms of social media reportage have been included in mainstream reportage as an alternative to the vox pop or survey, suggesting that 'what Twitter thinks' about an issue has now become a consistent feature of mainstream media coverage.

This convergence of interpersonal communication, individual broadcasting and networked engagement with news and information is key to understanding social media's influence on journalism. In these news environments, news is not formed through the subjective governance and structures prioritised by journalists and their news organisations, but rather through audience participation and engagement with particular topics and events. Audiences' public observation and sharing of events that represent 'news', as well as the active selection, filtering, commenting (Hermida et al. 2012) and sharing of news events created by others has changed the way news flows through social media environments and into public dialogue. In short, it is the dominance of online individual and community engagement with news events on social media that has been most disruptive to traditional news media production and publics. The ability of online audiences to either directly communicate with the producers of news, or to produce their own news, has influenced the ways in which news media organisations produce and distribute news.

Thus, the most obvious change brought by social media distribution of news is loss of control over the selection, timing and distribution of content to represent news events (Gillmor 2004). As Newman (2011, p. 10) suggests, legacy news media organisations are 'in a fight to maintain their control of distribution' because this maintains control over the representation of news events. This control has been replaced with precise data about social media audience preferences, as well as the influence of algorithmic filtering and prioritisation, resulting in news influenced less by journalistic agenda-setting and more by the number of audience shares or comments (see Chap. 5). Legacy news organisations are now competing with not just different news producers and stakeholders in online environments, but also the flows of likes, shares and recommendations from the users' social circles and the platform algorithms determining whether those likes, shares and recommendations should even be visible to the users.

This change in news distribution has been theorised as 'network journalism', where professional journalism operates as a node within a shared information environment alongside other stakeholders in the news (Deuze and Bardoel 2001). As Heinrich (2008) suggests, 'Within this evolving dense net of the information sphere, the opportunities to gather information have become immeasurable and so has the level of competition amongst an innumerable number of information providers'. Others have theorised journalism as belonging to a more broadly conceived media ecology, which takes into account the symbiotic relationship between people and their use and creation of media technologies—and how these systems impact on both personal and professional behaviours (Postman 1970, p. 161). Thus, an ecological approach prioritises communication as part of social life, but also emphasises the complex and multidirectional interactions between people, as well as the broader social, political and cultural contexts in which this communication occurs. While the conceptual understanding of these new production and distribution flows is not settled, it is clear that the effects of social media's technical and social affordances have resulted in a global flow of news and information characterised by multidirectional links between journalists, sources, audiences and other stakeholders in the news (Heinrich 2008). These multidirectional networks of news information flows, and the number of voices involved in its production and distribution, create somewhat chaotic and contingent networks that are non-linear but nonetheless interconnected (McNair 2006). As new affordances develop alongside new media business models and new user practices, opportunities for negotiation and experimentation will occur in conjunction with issues of news representation and labour. This has ramifications for journalism as an institution because it re-articulates the power of the journalist and the media organisation to set the daily news agenda. Instead, news events become subject to the interrelations between news organisations, journalists, individual users and online communities, who are now part of social media networks that connect and share content according to personal preference and relevance (Marwick and boyd 2011).

The commercial implication for news organisations is that they must compete with a vast pool of information and resources to be the most clicked news source. However, other studies have suggested that for news organisations savvy enough to work with social media flows of information, there are more opportunities to disseminate news to much larger and distributed audiences—and to divert greater numbers of eyes to embedded advertising. *Facebook* in particular, is a major competitor for embedded advertising online and news distribution on this platform can increase the number of users accessing both news and advertising

(Asur et al. 2011). While news organisations and online publishers have in the past relied mainly on *Google* for traffic through user search options, the emergence of social media as a distribution tool has changed the way news information flows online. Newman's (2011, p. 18) analysis of user access data for mainstream news organisations showed that the individual search is being usurped by growth in push services, such as links on social media. More recently, social media has become a news platform in and of itself, with news organisations concerned that their websites were becoming obsolete due to lack of user engagement. While news organisations benefit from the increased exposure of their content on social media, social media engagement with news actually draws eyes and clicks away from news organisations' websites and cuts into potential advertising revenue that pays for journalism (Asur et al. 2011). Yet both journalists and mainstream media organisations certainly work to promote, amplify and extend reportage of news stories using social media platforms. The amplification of a news event relies on social media interactions; that is, the complex interplay of both amateur and professional information about, and sharing of, new and existing information. This, in turn, allows for further verification, contextualisation and thus extended reporting of a news event. Thus, mainstream and social media forms of sourcing and distribution of news work together in complex symbiotic flows of information and engagement. These new interconnections undoubtedly create new issues for traditional journalistic practices, but they have also become integral to the distribution and amplification of news events. This interdependence also brings social and political interests to the representation of news itself and power struggles over who has the right to call a particular representation 'truth'.

Threats and Opportunities in a Post-Truth World

Perhaps the Trump-era focus on 'fake news' is an example of the duality of journalism in a social media age, illustrating just how far journalism has diverged from its institutional role, and yet how important some journalistic practices have become. Fake news has been described as demonstrably false statements made about people or events, as opposed to opinions or differing political perspectives. Most news audiences would be familiar with fake news through experience of news satire; websites like *The Onion* have been publishing satirical news pieces for many years (Mackey and Jacobson 2016). While the humorous intent is often obvious to readers, scholars and media pundits have suggested that as more people retrieve news from social media platforms, the division between 'real' and 'fake' news has sometimes been difficult to distinguish. Politically biased and fake news reporting on social media has manipulated these blurred distinctions by attempting to influence the news agenda and public opinion of particular issues. Fake news generally consists of fabricated reports, often about crimes against children or women, or a particular conspiracy theory. These 'reports' are often paired with particular political stakeholders attempting to lend credence (but not complicity) to these reports through sharing or liking on social media.

Fake news differs from hoax news, which has a long history in journalism (see Peters and Broersma 2013). Furthermore, hoax and fake news distribution is not a problem confined to social media; all communication technologies have been subject to manipulation, from H.G. Wells' famous fake 'War of the Worlds' radio broadcast (Bossio and Bebawi 2013) to the sacking of Australian newspaper columnist Paul Sheehan after printing an interviewee's false claims of rape by a 'Muslim gang' (Davidson 2016). Apart from attempting to manipulate representation of events for political or economic advantage, hoax news can also be satirical, or highlight issues in traditional media reportage. For example, an Australian production company called *The Woolshed* admitted in 2016 that it had created eight fake videos, including one of a man fighting off a shark and a woman almost getting hit by lightning (Crisp 2016). The videos went viral in over 180 countries and were watched 205 million times, but they were all part of an experiment, funded by *Screen Australia*, to better understand how to use social media techniques to create low-budget but highly popular content. While the company left clues about the dubious veracity of the videos, they were still shared on news websites and social media platforms, their virality illustrating the snowball effect of coverage around unverified media content. Thus, these hoaxes indicate that increasing digital literacy may not always assist users to identify fake news, especially as online and social media systems of production and distribution grow increasingly complex (Mackey and Jacobson 2016).

The most recently popularised iteration of fake news has not been for hoax or satire, but rather for politically strategic positioning. During the presidential campaign, Donald Trump utilised various lies; he denied that he had questioned Barack Obama's place of birth (Collinson and Diamond 2016), denied that he had publicly mocked a disabled reporter and denied that he had suggested, via *Twitter*, that one of his vocal critics, Alicia Machado, had a secret sex tape (Liebelson 2017; Jacobson 2016). Even on the first day of his administration, Trump lied about the number of people at his inauguration, saying there were in excess of one million people in attendance (Lee 2017). When this was shown to be demonstrably untrue, Counsellor to the President Kellyanne Conway, suggested that Trump's claims were 'alternative facts', while White House Press Secretary and Communications Director Sean Spicer suggested that 'sometimes we can disagree with the facts' (Meet the Press 2017; Smith 2017). So far during his administration, Trump has falsely suggested that his telephones were tapped by the Obama administration and repeated his campaign lie that he would have won the popular vote if three million illegal immigrants hadn't voted for Hillary Clinton (Trump Clings 2017; Liptak and Merica 2017).

Trump's lies before and after the election campaign were so flagrant that *Oxford Dictionaries* coined 'post-truth' as the 2016 word of the year (Word of the year 2016). The definition according to *Oxford Dictionaries* is 'relating to or denoting circumstances in which objective facts are less influential in shaping public opinion than appeals to emotion and personal belief' (Word of the year 2016). Perhaps the most acute example of this appeal to emotion was 'Pizzagate', the controversy surrounding a falsehood about Hillary Clinton that was propagated and distributed on far-right news media sites. 'Pizzagate' came to a dramatic climax when US police arrested a man who stormed a pizza restaurant that was supposedly the location of a child abuse ring led by Hillary Clinton. Despite the story being completely discredited, a link to the story was tweeted by General Mike Flynn, Donald Trump's first pick for national security adviser. In the month before the attack, General Flynn tweeted a link to the story with the comment 'U decide' (Washington Gunman 2016). Police claimed the man said he wanted to 'self-investigate' the so-called 'Pizzagate' scandal and attacked the restaurant with a rifle (Washington Gunman 2016). The owner of the restaurant had already received death threats and had publicly announced that the story was fake. In an age of social media reportage and distribution of news, 'Pizzagate' was its worst consequence. An audience member believed a fake news story that was strategically produced and distributed to discredit a presidential nominee and was given credibility on social media by a political stakeholder, rather than the practices of journalism. However, this audience member also believed so much in their own centrality within the news that they justified their own 'investigation' outside any of the legal or ethical norms of behaviour.

Despite the vigilante behaviour of the gunman, it is possible to understand how they might perceive themselves as justified in investigating information widely and uncritically shared on social media. Many of the characteristics of social media communication empower audience engagement with news based on shared interest in a topic, event or commercial activity. For many users, they are simply participating in information flows as part of a broader sense of 'digital citizenship': the participation and contribution to social and cultural life through the particular affordances of social media. On the other hand, this wider distribution opens up news events to many more stakeholders, as well as forms of aberrant behaviour, such as the vigilantism seen in 'Pizzagate', and forms of trolling, hoax content and misleading information. These 'negative' experiences also form part of the information flows on social media. While McCosker (2014, p. 202) suggests that these combative forms of behaviour are part of the formation of digital citizenship, these agonistic, incomplete and often unfinished flows of information on social media differ exponentially from the tightly governed, structured forms of communication created by traditional norms of professional journalism.

Trump's use of false accusations and claims about his governmental abilities, business achievements and policy success is unprecedented in political news reportage and has left many mainstream journalists and news organisations wondering how to report on both his election campaign and presidency. Traditional practices of reportage have been brought into sharp relief by the Trump administration; journalists have had to find ways to report the truth when a key political stakeholder blatantly lies, while ensuring that coverage of debunked lies does not detract from coverage of more important political issues. Furthermore, journalists and news organisations have been criticised both for reporting these lies and, conversely, for not publicly calling out lies when they occur. This suggests that it is not actually the fakery that is the issue—it is that a politician is flagrant in his disregard for the truth, and yet audiences disregard mainstream journalism's reporting of facts, or are more clearly swayed by emotional appeals, even if they are untrue. There might be social and political reasons for this, such as the growing economic divide and political disenchantment in the USA translating into political currency for any politician who promises disruption to the status quo. However, in the context of journalism, the disregard for mainstream reportage points to other issues, such as the lack of trust in mainstream media reportage enamoured with commercialised, aggregated, click bait-type news to the detriment of reportage for social benefit. Indeed, a persistent social criticism of institutionalised journalism is that it is disconnected from the audience—despite the characteristics of collaboration and engagement promoted by social media. An 'elite media' has been repeatedly criticised for being unrepresentative of public concerns; indeed, Muller (2016) suggests that 'The US media did seem to miss the [election] story comprehensively, but, in the process of debating why this happened, the word "elite" came to be used to describe a professional media that had lost democratic legitimacy'. If the criticism of mainstream journalism is that it has lost legitimacy as an institution, how has this arisen? The answer is perhaps in the new characteristics of communication that have defined social media culture and, thus, news production and consumption.

As more users rely on the affordances of social media to be informed about news—from news consumption practices based on individual discovery to practices based on recommendation and preference, the more likely it is that news will come from social media activities of sharing and user-driven processing (Bruns 2012, p. 99). While this could provide more diversity in news consumption, it may also lead to processes of commercialisation and homogenisation of news in order to appeal best to audiences. In Chap. 5, I discussed the opportunities and issues that occur in the practitioner and organisational use of algorithms to influence the distribution of news. The effects of prioritisation filters are not only that news organisations produce what is popular, but that audiences are also directed to content that algorithms choose for them, based on previous likes or engagement. That is, audiences only see what they 'like', rather than what is available. This creates what have been termed 'echo chambers': political and intellectual silos that are created when an algorithm's selective choices assume the news or information a user would want to engage with, allowing a user to avoid differing viewpoints. Similarly, this narrowing of the news agenda may also encourage homophilic tendencies in audience preference for connection with others who share their beliefs, rather than engaging in more diverse discussion. A study by *MIT* showed that these political silos were apparent during the 2016 US presidential election (Thompson 2016). The study used *Twitter's* social media data sets during the election to show that, rather than encouraging political debate, the characteristics of the platform encouraged different political groups, especially Trump supporters, to form insular groups with few connections to mainstream media (Thompson 2016). There was little information flow between political groups—or between the 'institutionalised media users that are supposed to be political discourse's immune system'. However, the research found that journalists were just as guilty as partisan users of separating themselves from political discussion—and were mostly disconnected from Trump supporters (Thompson 2016).

All these effects on the communication of news have left journalists with a 'post-truth' quandary of how to be balanced in the coverage of Trump's lies. Some news organisations have used euphemistic language to describe Trump's various lies, while others have decided to 'call out' each lie publicly. For example, a journalist at *BuzzFeed* suggests that reporting about Trump has created divergence in traditional reporting practices concerning his lies: 'Reporters are understandably cautious about using the word [lying]—some never do, because it requires speculating on what someone is thinking. The cases we call "lies" are ones where we think it's fair to make that call: Trump is saying something that contradicts clear and widely published information that we have reason to think he's seen' (Georgantopoulos 2017). Both positions have been criticised—one position obscures the 'truth' and the other obscures the analysis of policy in the public interest with the more sensationalist reporting of lies. The editor in chief of the *Wall Street Journal*, Gerard Baker (2017), invoked journalism's professional ideology to suggest that journalists should be reluctant to use the word 'lie' to describe Trump's utterances. He suggests that telling a reader 'in categorical terms that Trump had told a lie' would damage a journalist's professional reputation because 'to accuse someone of lying is to impute a wilful, deliberate attempt to deceive. It says he knowingly used a misrepresentation of the facts to mislead for his own purposes' (Baker 2017). Baker (2017) suggests that this imputation would require the journalist to have evidence of Trump's intent. Given that this evidence would be unlikely to be found, a journalist would otherwise be making a moral judgment, which would be seen by audiences as partisanship. Baker's (2017) appeal is thus to institutional norms of objectivity, suggesting Trump's appeals to emotion can only be countered with evidence and objectivity in order to earn the readers' trust.

Baker's suggestion was criticised by another journalist, Dan Rather, who also appealed to traditional, institutional ideals of journalism to suggest that 'It is not the proper role of journalists to meet lies, especially from someone of Mr. Trump's stature and power, by hiding behind semantics and euphemisms…When something is, in fact, a demonstrable lie, it is our responsibility to say so' (Erdman 2017). Where some have appealed to traditional notions of journalism and professionalism as a 'corrective' balance against fake news, others have argued for the use of social media techniques of transparency and collaboration. Some news organisations have argued for collaboration techniques across news organisations to ensure access to political stakeholders, and thus ensure they answer hard questions. For example, repeating questions asked by others but ignored at press conferences or collaborative data analysis has been suggested as a way to hold lying politicians to account.

There have also been a number of innovative journalistic responses to fake news that illustrate the productive potential of social media disruption to both journalistic authority and the practices of news production and distribution. An individual practitioner, Matt Kiser, who has worked in both journalism and social media analysis, has created *WTF Just happened today*, a daily analysis of the Trump administration's decisions and public discourse, which is compiled and emailed to subscribers. The site now has more than 48,000 newsletter subscribers with an open rate of over 50% (Kramer 2017). Similarly, larger news organisations have been utilising social media characteristics like sharing to counter fake news. For example, *BuzzFeed* is working on an interactive map of all the people and organisations that hold links to the Trump administration, using data analysis of public records, as well as asking the public to help find connections or context. Even legacy media are utilising a social media 'debunking' approach to Trump's administration; *The Washington Post* recently launched a 'Real Donald Context' plug-in for the *Google Chrome* browser, which fact-checks each of Trump's tweets (Machkovech 2016). Other news organisations have taken a broader approach to fact-checking. For example, the *BBC* takes a three-tiered approach to online and social media verification. The *BBC* writes regular 'myth-busting' articles about recent social and political events, running an internal fact-checking department, as well as working collaboratively with other media outlets to verify claims. Other online techniques of transparency and collaboration include Eli Pariser's use of collaborative solutions to counter fake news. Pariser used *Twitter* to launch a *Google Doc* called 'Design solutions for fake news' dedicated to reducing the impact of fake news, with hundreds of journalists and other contributors brainstorming strategies for identifying and tackling fake news (Morris 2016). While Pariser is not a journalist, he has now taken an interest in news storytelling, as the founder and CEO of *Upworthy*, a site dedicated to using virality to promote political and social issues. While the site began by aggregating content from other sites, it now employs journalists and media producers to create original content.

Eli Pariser's collaborative, crowdsourced attempts to counter the influence of fake news are perhaps a way to envision the journalism of the future. While there is no doubt that those media organisations investing in online and social media-enabled technologies will increasingly utilise opportunities such as artificial intelligence (AI), big data and algorithms, these will also come with social and institutional effects on journalism. Journalists will need to work alongside other stakeholders in the news agenda, and with the constantly evolving information flows created by new modes of news production and distribution to ensure that journalism's professional practice continues to have a social impact. If the heart of journalism is public dialogue—finding news and information that inspire and maintain communication practices in the service of public interests—then journalism is still needed. But if the nature of public dialogue is changing, the institutional boundaries of journalism must change with it. The collaborative, transparent and inclusive public interest projects that serve to highlight fake news illustrate how the evolution of journalism's institutional boundaries might benefit public dialogue.

Conclusion

The speed of the distribution of news and information, through sharing, liking and other forms of prioritisation on social media, has had many positive impacts, especially on social justice issues have gained international momentum through social media engagement. Nonetheless, many of these positive effects have been outweighed by coverage of the problematic use of social media—outcomes such as trolling, hoaxes and, of course, the onset of social media-disseminated 'fake news' have become characteristic calling cards of social media use and distribution of information. The use of fake news as a political tool has been a source of concern in other countries too. Fake news and alleged Russian interference in election campaigns—either by influencing fake news sites or by producing misinformation—have been reported as serious concerns in the lead-up to the German elections. The most obvious example of fake news in Germany was a report that Middle Eastern refugees had gang-raped a 13-year-old Russian girl in Berlin (McGuiness 2016). The story received extensive coverage in Russian and German media but Berlin's chief of police indicated that the news was fabricated. This did not stop the story being widely shared on social media, concluding in a large-scale protest in Berlin and a politicised rebuke by Russia's foreign minister, who suggested that the news had been ignored by Angela Merkel's government (McGuiness 2016). Like many of these fake news reports, the content is blatantly racist or misogynistic and plays on fears of an attack on traditional principles or innocent children or (Caucasian) women.

Professional practices that allow journalists to expose and report information on behalf of the public, often by doing the long and tedious work of research and interviews, are still needed. The boundaries that shape how these professional practices are executed may have changed, but the need for someone to do this work while adhering to ethical and legal boundaries of that labour is still important. Muller (2016) suggests that professionalised and institutionalised journalism still has a place in the public sphere and in the public interest:

> Journalism…is a complex exercise demanding skill and experience. Yes, professional journalism has many flaws and neither the practitioners nor the media industry they work for are as accountable as they should be for the way they use their power. But there is some accountability, including some serious legal consequences. Moreover, they operate in the open, with no cloak of anonymity to hide behind. This is the kind of journalism that serves the public interest.

While the traditionally rigid boundaries that fence in journalism's professional practices have served to maintain their social power in the past, the new production and distribution methods enabled by social media are in danger of fencing journalism out of public dialogue. Indeed, political squabbles over fake news have not worked in favour of public dialogue, only serving to highlight how easily other stakeholders in the news agenda can exert influence over social media news flows. However, these squabbles have also served to compound efforts to focus journalism on what has always been its original goal—to facilitate public dialogue by doing the hard work of shining a light on the public record.

The news-making and distribution processes will only continue to change as new social media platforms are introduced and existing platforms develop particular cultures of use. The adoption of any change to the news-making process, of course, ultimately relies on the engagement and adoption by users and news audiences. It is the individual user that ultimately adopts new practices and platform allegiances. As they find new practices to filter, block and like relevant content, news organisations and their journalists will also have to shift to accommodate these new preferences. The interconnections between the practices of individual journalists, the news organisations that support them and the institutions that frame their social role must be flexible, as new affordances on new platforms increasingly influence modes of production and distribution of news.

References

Aday, S., Livingston, S., & Hebert, M. (2005). Embedding the truth: A cross-cultural analysis of objectivity and television coverage of the Iraq war. *Harvard International Journal of Press/Politics, 10*(1), 3–21.

Asur, S., Huberman, B. A., Szabo, G., & Wang, C. (2011). Trends in social media: Persistence and decay. *HP Labs*. Retrieved from http://www.scribd.com/doc/48665388/Trends-in-Social-Media-Persistence-and-Decay.

Baker, G. (2017, January 6). Trump, lies and the challenge for traditional, honest journalism. *The Australian*. Retrieved from http://www.theaustralian.com.au/business/wall-street-journal/trump-lies-and-the-challenge-for-honest-traditional-journalism/news-story/4c14ec8ba7896a026a31d52619e5e61f.

Bossio, D., & Bebawi, S (2013). War of Worlds? Alternative and mainstream journalistic practices in coverage of the 'Arab Spring' protests. In J.E. Hayes, K. Battles & W. Hilton-Morrow (Eds.), *War of the words to social media: Mediated communication in times of crisis* (pp. 189–211). USA: Peter Lang.

Bruns, A. (2012). Journalists and Twitter: How Australian news organisations adapt to a new medium. *Media International Australia, 144*(1), 97–107.

Burgess, J., & Bruns, A. (2012). Researching news discussion on social media: New methodologies. *Journalism Studies, 13*(5–6), 801–814.

Collinson, S., & Diamond, J. (2016, September 16). Trump finally admits it: 'President Barack Obama was born in the United States'. *CNN*. Retrieved from http://edition.cnn.com/2016/09/15/politics/donald-trump-obama-birther-united-states/.

Crisp, A. (2016, July 11). How a small Melbourne production company fooled the world—Eight times. *Mumbrella*. Retrieved from https://mumbrella.com.au/melbourne-production-company-social-media-viral-fooled-world-8-times-379214.

Davidson, D. (2016, March 4). Paul Sheehan stood down from Fairfax after fake rape column. *The Australian*. Retrieved from http://www.theaustralian.com.au/business/media/paul-sheehan-stood-down-from-fairfax-after-fake-rape-column/news-story/2d58e0d4ba636a99e248f5429cf97362.

Deuze, M., & Bardoel, J. (2001). Network journalism: Converging competences of media professionals and professionalism. *Australian Journalism Review, 23*(2), 91–103.

Erdman, S. (2017, January 4). Dan Rather calls out Wall Street Journal over not calling Trump's lies 'lies'. *Fox 25 Boston*. Retrieved from http://www.fox25boston.com/news/dan-rather-calls-out-wall-street-journal-over-not-calling-trumps-lies-lies/481252104.

Georgantopoulos, M. (2017, January 27). Here's a running list of President Trump's lies and other bullshit. *Buzzfeed*. Retrieved from https://www.buzzfeed.com/maryanngeorgantopoulos/president-trump-lie-list?utm_=&utm_term=.tbR0gQ01v#.vsjXBqXpy.

Gillmor, D. (2004). *We the media: Grassroots journalism by the people, for the people*. Sebastopol, CA: O'Reilly Media.

Heinrich, A. (2008, October). *Network journalism: Moving towards a global journalism culture*. Paper presented at the RIPE conference 'Public Service Media for Communication and Partnership', Mainz, Germany. Retrieved from http://citeseerx.ist.psu.edu/viewdoc/download?doi=10.1.1.662.5360&rep=rep1&type=pdf.

Hermida, A., Fletcher, F., Korell, D., & Logan, D. (2012). Share, like, recommend: Decoding the social media news consumer. *Journalism Studies, 13*(5–6), 815–824.

Jacobson, L. (2016, October 9). Trump's pants on fire about his early morning tweet on Alicia Machado. *Politifact*. Retrieved from http://www.politifact.com/truth-o-meter/statements/2016/oct/09/donald-trump/trump-early-morning-sex-tape-tweet/.

Kramer, M. (2017, February 14). Meet the wildly popular blogger chronicling President Trump one day at a time. *Poynter*. Retrieved from https://www.poynter.org/2017/meet-the-wildly-popular-blogger-chronicling-president-trump-one-day-at-a-time/448894/.

Lee, T. B. (2017, January 23). Trump says 1.5 million people came to his inauguration. Here's what the evidence shows. *Vox*. Retrieved from http://www.vox.com/policy-and-politics/2017/1/21/14347298/trump-inauguration-crowd-size.

Liebelson, D. (2017, January 10). Donald Trump denies mocking a disabled reporter, even though it appears he did. *Huffington Post*. Retrieved from http://www.huffingtonpost.com.au/entry/donald-trump-reporter-disability_us_58738c2fe4b043ad97e473f2.

Liptak, K., & Merica, D. (2017, January 25). Trump believes millions voted illegally, WH says—But provides no proof. *CNN*. Retrieved from http://edition.cnn.com/2017/01/24/politics/wh-trump-believes-millions-voted-illegally/.

Machkovech, S. (2016, December 17). Washington Post automatically inserts Trump fact-checks into Twitter. *Arstechnica*. Retrieved from https://arstechnica.com/tech-policy/2016/12/washington-post-automatically-inserts-trump-fact-checks-into-twitter/.

Mackey, P., & Jacobson, T. (2016, December 6). How can we learn to reject fake news in the digital world? *The Conversation*. Retrieved February 8, 2017, from https://theconversation.com/how-can-we-learn-to-reject-fake-news-in-the-digital-world-69706.

Marwick, A. E., & boyd, d. (2011). I tweet honestly, I tweet passionately: Twitter users, context collapse, and the imagined audience. *New Media & Society, 13*(1), 114–133.

McCosker, A. (2014). Trolling as provocation: YouTube's agonistic publics. *Convergence: The International Journal of Research into New Media Technologies, 20*(2), 201–217.

McNair, B. (2006). *Cultural chaos: journalism and power in a globalised world*. Abingdon, OX: Routledge.

McGuiness, D. (2016, January 27). Russia steps into Berlin 'rape' storm claiming German cover-up. *BBC*. Retrieved from http://www.bbc.com/news/blogs-eu-35413134.

Meet The Press with Chuck Todd. (2017, January 22). *NBC*. Retrieved from http://www.nbcnews.com/meet-the-press/video/conway-press-secretary-gave-alternative-facts-860142147643.

Morris, D. (2016, November 28). Eli Pariser's fake news brain trust is tackling fake news. *Fortune*. Retrieved from http://fortune.com/2016/11/27/eli-pariser-fake-news-brain-trust/.

Muller, D. (2016, December 9). You say 'elite media', I say real journalism. And now more than ever we must fight to keep it. *The Conversation*. Retrieved February 8, 2017, from https://theconversation.com/you-say-elite-media-i-say-real-journalism-and-now-more-than-ever-we-must-fight-to-keep-it-69975.

Newman, N. (2011). Mainstream media and the distribution of news in the age of social discovery: How social media are changing the production, distribution and discovery of news and further disrupting the business models of mainstream media companies. *Reuters Institute for the Study of Journalism*. Retrieved from http://reutersinstitute.politics.ox.ac.uk/fileadmin/documents/Publications/The_rise_of_social_media_and_its_365impact_on_mainstream_journalism.pdf.

Pape, S., & Featherstone, S. (2005). *Newspaper journalism: A practical introduction*. London: Sage.

Peters, C., & Broersma, M. J. (Eds.). (2013). *Rethinking journalism: Trust and participation in a transformed news landscape*. Routledge.

Postman, N. (1970). The Reformed English Curriculum. In A.C Eurich. (Ed.), *High school 1980: the shape of the future in American secondary education* (pp. 160–168). New York: Pittman Publishing.

Robinson, P. (2005). *The CNN effect: The myth of news, foreign policy and intervention*. London: Routledge.

Smith, D. (2017, January 24). Sean Spicer defends inauguration claim: 'Sometimes we can disagree with facts'. *The Guardian*. Retrieved from https://www.theguardian.com/us-news/2017/jan/23/sean-spicer-white-house-press-briefing-inauguration-alternative-facts.

Thompson, A. (2016, December 8). Parallel narratives: Clinton and Trump supporters really don't listen to each other on Twitter. *Vice*. Retrieved from https://news.vice.com/story/journalists-and-trump-voters-live-in-separate-online-bubbles-mit-analysis-shows.

Trump clings to Obama wiretapping claims. (2017, March 18). *SBS*. Retrieved from http://www.sbs.com.au/news/article/2017/03/18/trump-clings-obama-wiretapping-claims.

Washington gunman motivated by fake news 'Pizzagate' conspiracy. (2016, December 5). *The Guardian*. Retrieved from https://www.theguardian.com/us-news/2016/dec/05/gunman-detained-at-comet-pizza-restaurant-was-self-investigating-fake-news-reports.

Word of the year 2016 is.... (2016). *Oxford living dictionaries*. Retrieved from https://en.oxforddictionaries.com/word-of-the-year/word-of-the-year-2016.

CHAPTER 8

Conclusion: Where to from Here for Professional Journalism?

In April 2017, the first of the French presidential elections was held amidst much controversy. The front-runners for election, Marine Le Pen and the subsequent winner of the first round of votes, Emmanuel Macron, represent the far-right and centre-right of French politics respectively. Le Pen, as the president of the *National Front*, campaigned similarly to Donald Trump, prioritising nationalistic policies such as curbing immigration and exiting the eurozone. Her campaign has also been dogged by judicial inquiries into her business and political associates, with many in the media questioning the appropriateness of her political choices and potential conflicts of interest. Perhaps the most troubling aspect of the campaign was the claims of US-style fake news infiltrating the media reportage about the elections. The use of 'junk news', automated through dissemination algorithms or bots that promote specific content, has been a significant part of so-called 'computational propaganda' used during the French elections. Indeed, the *World Economic Forum* (2014) has previously presented this automated misinformation as one of the top ten perils to society. In Chap. 7, the manipulation of news and information by state and non-state actors was discussed: 'fake news' distributed via social media platforms for the purpose of deliberately misleading the public for political gain. Despite the often obvious fakery, these pieces of news attract web traffic and drive engagement and therefore influence public dialogue and demobilise genuine critical engagement with political and social life.

D. Bossio, *Journalism and Social Media*,
DOI 10.1007/978-3-319-65472-0_8

Within a 'post-truth' environment of communication, Mihailidis and Viotty (2017) suggest fake and junk news are driven by 'an increasingly polarised and distrustful public spending an increasing amount of time in homophilous networks' empowered by the spreadability, connectivity and spectacle engendered by social media platforms. However, they suggest these issues are not caused by lack of media availability. Just as the introduction of social media to journalism is not simply about the technology itself, the solutions to the social, political and organisational issues raised by increasing social media use are not just technological in nature. Indeed, as the era of fake news has developed, so too have the innovative media production and consumption habits of producers and audiences. Both journalists and audiences have negotiated a number of different solutions, both social and technical, to combat the issue.

This was particularly obvious during the French election, when research conducted by the *Oxford Internet Institute* indicated that, on average, 7.2% of social media content about French politics was generated by bots, which increased slightly as the campaign progressed (Howard et al. 2017, p. 3). However, while French users appeared to be sharing more junk news in comparison with their German counterparts talking about the upcoming German elections, public dialogue did not appear to be as tainted by fake or junk news. In comparison, the researchers found a 1:1 ratio between professional news content and junk news in the lead up to the US election, compared with 4:1 for Germans (Howard et al. 2017, p. 4). The ratio for social media users in France was in the middle at 2:1. However, French voters seemed to be sharing better quality information than in the USA. This suggests the dynamism and variability of news production and consumption on social media, where constant change in the use of social media is only outpaced by the changes in the consumption habits of audiences.

In the context of the development of professional journalism, one thing has remained constant. The largest proportion of content shared on social media about the election came from professional news organisations (Howard et al. 2017, p. 3). The 20% of content that was not professionally produced news did not actually come from junk news, but from citizen-generated content (Howard et al. 2017, p. 3). This corresponds to recent research that has shown audiences still place their trust (and their clicks) in legacy news media both online and on social media. Dodds and Vir (2016) showed that online audiences go to the websites of well-established, often legacy, news organisations to learn about news stories and gather key facts. This research showed that established and trusted news brands are still perceived as playing a valuable social role, but the visibility of these brands varied for different audience demographics; the younger the audience, the more likely it would be that initial awareness of news would come from social media (Dodds & Vir 2016). Therefore, legacy news media still claims an important role in informing the public, but on social media, its reach and influence is much more fragmented. Similarly, professional journalists and trusted news brands also still play a valuable social role, but the visibility of professional journalism varies across social media environments. Thus, the characteristic social and cultural affordances of social media have impacted new modes of communication as well as new ways of producing and sharing news.

This book has conceptualised these changing modes of journalistic practice and influence across interconnected links between individual practitioners, organisational structure and institutional understanding of journalism. I have argued that the impact of social media on journalism can be seen through the complex and interconnected relations, practices and professional boundaries between individual practitioners, news organisations and institutional understandings of journalism that seek both to innovate and delimit the ways in which social media can be used in a news context. This book has sought to critically analyse the impact of these interconnected influences through the opportunities and challenges that have emerged for practitioners, organisations and the profession overall as a result of the increasing use of social media in reportage. To do so, the chapters in this book have analysed how the characteristics of social media communication influence—and are influenced by—new journalistic practices, new relations with audiences, organisational processes and models of news distribution, as well as the institutional characteristics of journalism and news overall.

In Chap. 2, the influence of social media on individual journalistic practices was discussed. Focussing on three seemingly inviolable norms of professional journalism practice—objectivity, verification and autonomy—I argued that online modes of interaction prioritising authenticity, transparency and collaborative representation of news are having an impact on these traditional modes of practice. Tracing some of the influences on individual practice, these shifts are seen as occurring in response to new forms of content distribution, as well as new forms of interactivity and engagement with news content on social media. Nonetheless, this chapter showed that this influence was not a fait accompli, but was symptomatic of a profession in a state of transition. Having focussed for so many years on the traits and behaviours that define professional journalism and its social and cultural authority, the disruptive influence of online and social media cultures on the discursive authority of mainstream journalism has encouraged practitioners to reconsider both their professional methodologies and social role. Currently, news audiences are seeing the product of some experimentation in the mainstream media, including: more use of eyewitness accounts sourced from social media interactions; more professional branding activities on social media platforms; and more interest in collaborative and curatorial approaches to journalistic practice. Collaboration is one of the key practices enabled by social media and its journalistic use is increasing. In 2010, *Democracy Fund* documented more than 30 journalism collaborations occurring across international journalism (Kramer 2017). In less than ten years, this number has more than doubled and is increasingly enabled by social media platforms and affordances. Nonetheless, a number of different professional interests, organisational policies, and social, cultural and political norms continue to delimit the ways journalists are able to practise and thus the professional project of 'boundary keeping' continues—professional journalists may experiment discursively, but their hard-won professional 'insider' status is not easily given up. Thus, it is the journalists' relationship with the various distributed news audiences that will perhaps most likely indicate how professional journalism ends up situating itself in the public sphere.

In this period of transition, many journalists are negotiating new modes of communication, often having to unlearn many of the practices and behaviours instilled by professional and institutional norms. Hare (2017) suggests that stagnant organisational cultures, outdated practices for researching and producing news, and misconceptions about the audience need to change. More importantly, learning new skills should prioritise increasing the possibilities for public dialogue as an outcome, rather than more simplistic or quantified measures of professional or organisational popularity. These changing modes of journalistic professional behaviour and production are contextualised in Chap. 3, through the interactions between journalists and online publics that access news in social media environments. This chapter illustrates the empowerment of audiences on social media and the dominance of their preferences in the production and consumption of news. Thus, the traditional journalistic conception of the audience as a unified mass to which news and information should be broadcast has been replaced by highly distributed networks of issue-oriented audiences on social media. I argued that it is thus not only journalistic practice that is changing in an era of social media, but also the nature of public dialogue and, subsequently, the framework for professional journalism's importance in social life.

While the first part of the book focussed on the interrelations between journalists and their audiences, the second part of the book prioritised the often unacknowledged organisational structures, processes and relationships that delimit the ways in which social media can be used by journalists to innovate their practice. Chapter 4 focussed on the transition of journalistic production and distribution of news from an organisational perspective—in particular, the new professional relationships, policies and procedures that have been introduced to govern both the individual and organisational use of social media in the newsroom. This chapter thus illustrated Boczkowski's (2004) argument that organisational structures and associated processes of structuring journalistic labour influence how technologies are individually adopted, mediated through organisational strategies for use, and understandings of audience and, finally, journalism's professional culture. In utilising social media, both the technologies themselves and the relations between the various newsroom stakeholders shape both innovative and resistant practices.

While Chap. 4 focussed on the relationships that create the culture of social media use in the newsroom, Chap. 5 extended this discussion, tracing the use of data and algorithms in journalism, from the introduction of computer-assisted reporting to the more recent use of social media analytics. This chapter argued that an important new challenge for journalism is the manipulation of social media algorithms by other social and political stakeholders, especially those that focus on prioritisation and filtering of news to influence audience consumption. Indeed, new forms of algorithmic and automated journalism place the journalist on a par with machine-operated methodologies of producing journalism—or bypass journalists altogether. Nonetheless, the use of algorithms highlighted a paradox that both journalistic and algorithmic practice share. Similarly to journalism, organisational use of algorithms is represented through the norm of objectivity, which serves both to legitimise its social authority and suggest the credibility of its product. However, as Cheney-Leopold (2011, p. 165) argues, algorithms go one step further: where journalism condenses users into one unified mass, the technological capabilities enabling both data tracking and associated 'sense-making' of user habits construct and subsequently commercialise inferred identities onto individual users. Thus, both journalistic and algorithmic practices show the sociopolitical frameworks and relationships that underpin their strategic positioning in the public sphere; indeed, the outcomes of both the Brexit referendum and the US election showed the social significance not just of the use of audience analytics, but the potential manipulation of audience news consumption.

Indeed, for all the influence that audiences now have in social media-enabled news environments, it is surprising how little their needs factor in the actual production of content—quite apart from the analysis of what might be popular online. It is this confusion between the editorial and strategic priorities of legacy news organisations that encourages distrust of professional journalism. This distrust, coupled with the empowerment that social media modes of communication give audiences to find and investigate their own information, can be the catalyst not just for charges of media elitism against contemporary journalism, but also for dangerous political scenarios like 'Pizzagate'. The major issue for social media environments is not necessarily media literacy: it is the suspicion, now held by new audiences, that legacy news organisations desperate for clicks are trying to sell them something other than news. While most journalists have re-learned skills that enable them to work in online and social media environments, including optimising their content for speed, interactivity and engagement, 'optimising for trust' will continue to be a key institutional norm for professional journalism (Albeanu 2017). Many of the transitions in journalistic practice that incorporate collaboration and transparency are part of improving trust of professional journalism practices in online spaces.

The last part of the book broadens the focus to institutional framing of journalism. Changes to journalism practices, whether in relation to reporting, audience engagement or organisational structures, all have a larger impact on the constitution of journalism: how journalists think about the way they do their job and its importance in social and cultural life. Chapter 6 explored how journalists are balancing individual, organisational and professional norms while attempting to transition journalistic professional activity into social media environments. Looking at the way journalists represent their personal and professional identities on social media, this chapter argued that journalists' presentation strategies on social media were the manifestation of institutional change in journalism. That is, the ways journalists present their personal and professional identities on social media platforms correspond to some of the complex influences they are trying to balance while attempting to change their practices.

Finally, Chap. 7 considered the changes that social media use has brought to the constitution of news and disruptions to journalism's institutional authority to represent 'truth'. In 2017, we are now living in what has been called a 'post-truth' world in which journalists and audiences have had to continually negotiate what can be understood as 'true'. I argued that new modes of producing news and new business models for distributing news have resulted in the decentralisation of the journalist and news organisation from the communication of news. The introduction of social media into the distribution processes of news has been—and continues to be—disruptive to traditional news-making processes. The promise of social media was the re-invigoration of the public sphere through new distribution networks and prominence given to user creation and engagement. Social media was meant to help re-vitalise social values by sharing and discussing news as part of a burgeoning digital democracy. The reality has been rather more complicated. Social media has brought speed and global reach to mainstream media organisations, niche news providers, journalists and individual social media users, resulting in a complex interdependence that brings global attention and action to important social and political issues. This means that there are now more stakeholders in the selection and distribution of news and, in a post-truth world, this has meant the continual negotiation of representations of truth and the right to determine how it is distributed to audiences.

Thus, social media has contributed to the changing constitution of journalism through the creation of new cultures of communication, within which the roles of participants and the rules of engagement are still being negotiated. Social media cultures of communication, with their prioritisation of affective content based on personal opinion and experience and, finally, the centrality of the user in the construction of ad hoc publics engaged with issues and events of interest create public spaces and communities with very different cultures, politics and rules of civil engagement. Indeed, participants in such complex and distributed online publics collectively negotiate the roles—and rules—of social relations in these spaces, with these negotiations unfolding through both positive and negative feedback (Shaw et al. 2013, p. 26). Participation in the intimate relations of social media communication does not always adhere to the traditional rules of journalism. Greater opportunities to collaborate and represent diverse viewpoints using the various affordances of social media are coupled with the tensions created by other social and political stakeholders with interests in influencing what news, and journalism, should be.

A limitation of this book, amongst many others, is that it does not present an answer to the question of what journalism will look like in a post-truth world—nor, indeed, further into the future. Instead, this book has presented journalism as a profession in transition; while there are a number of practices, business models and news products that have shown innovative responses to the introduction of social media, there is just as much resistance to changes that stray too far from journalism's professional ideology. While change is slow and incremental, it is, nonetheless, going to impact on the role and practice of journalism in future. If we are looking to understand how the future of journalism will be framed in a post-truth world, perhaps the best place to start is with future news consumers. The *Knight Foundation*'s research into how young people navigate news environments indicated that many young adults experience and navigates news in completely different ways from previous generations (Madden et al. 2017). The report found that young people experience news as part of the ambient buzz of information they encounter as they flow through (rather than search for) social media content. As the report suggests, 'young people don't follow the news as much as it follows them' (Madden et al. 2017, p. 4). More importantly, the boundaries of what constituted news were permeable and deeply influenced by particular characteristics and uses of social media platforms. In social media environments, news is experienced through the affordances of social media platforms themselves; content is encountered through serendipity and in interstitial moments, as young people dip in and out of the flows of news across various platforms (Madden et al. 2017, p. 20). News in this environment is usually amorphous and extends beyond the content produced by traditional journalistic institutions. Many of the participants suggested a distrust of news media, instead placing value on the reputation of the individual sharing the news. Despite the lack of trust in the news media, young adults wanted to know about current events and sought out multiple sources to understand them. Many suggested that they valued media that prioritised transparency in reporting and coverage of news relevant to their lives (Madden et al. 2017, p. 20).

This research parallels much of what this book has suggested about the development and future of journalism in a social media age. The role of journalism in social life will develop alongside technological changes, as it always has, but in order to continue to provide social value, journalism must also evolve as an institution. With millions of voices crying out for attention, and a million different vested interests in holding it, social media has provided a way to access some voices, and to filter out others. As a result, social media publics have become complex, interconnected and, increasingly, problematic. Users find that news spaces require new and different etiquettes, discursive politics and, even, representations of truth. Furthermore, the seemingly 'porous' legal and ethical frameworks for social media use, the distributed nature of social media content and the ever-changing political and social uses of different platforms have all illustrated that the way in which news and information flows through social media has an impact on public discourse.

Journalism and professional journalists both have a place within social media's future, but how it is constituted as a practice and social institution will change. Approaches dominated by autonomy and broadcast communication practices will be replaced by collaboration and networked communication. Organisations dominated by hierarchical decision-making and rigid business structures will be replaced by small, lean workplaces populated by multiskilled media producers, community managers and technical staff. Finally, journalism as an institution must change in order to have the social influence that characterises its ideological framework and norms of behaviour. This book has illustrated the different ways in which social media impacts and is impacted by professional journalistic practice, as well as the organisations and institutions that produce, distribute and structure those practices. It has shown that journalists are competing with far more voices in the public sphere in order to distribute representations of news and information. The target of news—the audience—has varied media literacy skills, access and interests in engaging with these various representations of news. In between the journalist and the audience are the various organisational, political, social and cultural influences that seek to structure, regulate and influence the ways in which news is produced and understood. Thus, the introduction of social media to journalism is not simply about social or technical tools for the production of news, but rather, as always, the relations between them, and how these create the possibilities for producing and sharing news and information.

References

Albeanu, C. (2017, April 8). Optimising for trust: Advice for news organisations to improve their relationship with the public. *Journalism.co.uk*. Retrieved from https://www.journalism.co.uk/news/optimising-for-trust-advice-for-news-organisations-to-improve-their-relationship-with-the-public/s2/a702368/.

Boczkowski, P. (2004). The processes of adopting multimedia and interactivity in three online newsrooms. *Journal of Communication, 54*(2), 197–213.

Cheney-Lippold, J. (2011). A new algorithmic identity: Soft biopolitics and the modulation of control. *Theory, Culture & Society, 28*(6), 164–181.

Dodds, A., & Vir, J. (2016). The future for news brands in an increasingly distributed and fragmented world. *Reuters Institute for the study of Journalism*. Retrieved from http://digitalnewsreport.org/essays/2016/future-news-brands-increasingly-distributed-fragmented-world/.

Hare, K. (2017, April 18). Local Edition: What do journalists need to stop doing to survive? *Poynter*. Retrieved from http://www.poynter.org/2017/local-edition-what-do-journalists-need-to-stop-doing-to-survive/456300/.

Howard, P. N., Bradshaw, S., Kollanyi, B., Desigaud, C., & Bolsover, G. (2017). Junk News and bots during the French Presidential Election: What are French voters sharing over Twitter? *Comprop Data Memo*. Retrieved from http://comprop.oii.ox.ac.uk/wp-content/uploads/sites/89/2017/04/What-Are-French-Voters-Sharing-Over-Twitter-v9.pdf.

Kramer, M. (2017, February 14). Meet the wildly popular blogger chronicling President Trump one day at a time. *Poynter*. Retrieved from https://www.poynter.org/2017/meet-the-wildly-popular-blogger-chronicling-president-trump-one-day-at-a-time/448894/.

Madden, M., Lenhart, A., & Fontaine, C. (2017). How youth navigate the news landscape. *Knight Foundation*. Retrieved from https://kf-site-production.s3.amazonaws.com/publications/pdfs/000/000/230/original/Youth_News.pdf.

Mihailidis, P., & Viotty, S. (2017). Spreadable spectacle in digital culture: Civic expression, fake news and the role of media literacies in 'post-fact' society. *American Behavioural Science*. Retrieved from http://journals.sagepub.com/doi/abs/10.1177/0002764217701217?journalCode=absb.

Shaw, F., Burgess, J., Crawford, K., & Bruns, A. (2013). Sharing news, making sense, saying thanks. *Australian Journal of Communication*. *40*(1) , 23–39.

World Economic Forum. (2014). The rapid spread of misinformation online. *Outlook on the Global Agenda*. Retrieved from http://reports.weforum.org/outlook-14/top-ten-trends-category-page/10-the-rapid-spread-of-misinformation-online/.

Bibliography

Atton, C. (2002). *Alternative Media*. London: Sage.

Brill, A. M. (2001). Online journalists embrace new marketing function. *Newspaper Research Journal, 22*(2), 28–40.

Burns, A. (2010). Oblique strategies for ambient journalism. *Media-Culture Journal, 13*(2). Retrieved from http://journal.mediaculture.org.au/index.php/mcjournal/article/view/Article/23.

Bruns, A. (2011). A first map of Australia. *Mapping Online Publics*. Retrieved from http://www.mappingonlinepublics.net/2011/08/04/a-first-map-of-australia/.

Burgess, J. (2015). From 'broadcast yourself' to 'follow your interests': Making over social media. *International Journal of Cultural Studies, 18*(3), 281–285.

Chadwick, A. (2013). *The hybrid media system: Politics and power*. Oxford, UK: Oxford University Press.

Cooper, T. (1990). Comparative international media ethics. *Journal of Mass Media Ethics, 5*(1), 3–14.

Kovach, B., & Rosenstiel, T. (2007). *The elements of journalism: What newspeople should know and the public should expect*. New York: Three Rivers Press.

Pariser, E. (2011). *The filter bubble: What the Internet is hiding from you*. UK: Penguin.

Rosen, J. (2004, January 7). Journalism is itself a religion: Special essay on launch of The Revealer. *PressThink*. Retrieved from http://archive.pressthink.org/2004/01/07/press_religion_p.html.

Rutenberg, J. (2016, August 7). Trust is testing the norms of objectivity in Journalism. *The New York Times*. Retrieved from http://www.nytimes.com/2016/08/08/business/balance-fairness-and-a-proudly-provocative-presidential-candidate.html.

D. Bossio, *Journalism and Social Media*,
DOI 10.1007/978-3-319-65472-0

Schudson, M. (2001). The objectivity norm in American journalism. *Journalism, 2*(2), 149–170.

Singer, J., Domingo, D., Heinonen, A., Hermida, A., Paulussen, S., Quandt, T., et al. (2011). *Participatory journalism: Guarding open gates at online newspapers.* USA: Wiley-Blackwell.

Index

D. Bossio, *Journalism and Social Media*,
DOI 10.1007/978-3-319-65472-0

O

P

Q

R

FSC
www.fsc.org
MIX
Papier | Fördert
gute Waldnutzung
FSC® C083411

Kolibri 360 GmbH
Ferdinand-Jühlke-Straße 7
99095 Erfurt, Deutschland
produktsicherheit@kolibri360.de